Roger W. Moss

THE AMERICAN COUNTRY HOUSE

Henry Holt and Company   New York

Copyright © 1990 by LCA Associates
Published by Henry Holt and Company, Inc.,
115 West 18th Street, New York, New York 10011.
Published in Canada by Fitzhenry & Whiteside Limited,
195 Allstate Parkway, Markham, Ontario L3R 4T8.

Library of Congress Cataloging-in-Publication Data
Moss, Roger W., 1940–
The American country house / Roger W. Moss — 1st ed.
    p.   cm.
Includes bibliographical references.
ISBN 0-8050-1248-6 (alk. paper)
1. Country homes — United States.   2. Mansions — United States.
I. Title.
NA7561.M67   1991   90-4362
728.8'0973 — dc20   CIP

Henry Holt books are available at special discounts
for bulk purchases for sales promotions, premiums,
fund-raising, or educational use. Special editions
or book excerpts can also be created to specification.
For details contact:
Special Sales Director, Henry Holt and Company, Inc.,
115 West 18th Street New York, New York 10011.

FIRST EDITION

Designed by Joy Chu

Printed in the United States of America
Recognizing the importance of preserving the written word
Henry Holt and Company, Inc., by policy, prints all of its
first editions on acid-free paper.∞

10 9 8 7 6 5 4 3 2 1

Grateful acknowledgment is made for permission to reproduce
a still from *Gone With the Wind* (page 8). Copyright 1939
by Selznick International Pictures, Inc., renewed © 1967
by Metro-Goldwyn-Mayer, Inc.

THIS BOOK IS DEDICATED TO

THOSE STEADFAST OWNERS

OF PRIVATE AMERICAN COUNTRY HOUSES

WHO DAILY DO BATTLE WITH THE HYDRA OF

SKYROCKETING MAINTENANCE,

UNSKILLED MECHANICS,

CONFISCATORY TAXES,

GREEDY DEVELOPERS,

OFFICIAL INDIFFERENCE,

AND PUBLIC SLOTH.

CONTENTS

THE AMERICAN COUNTRY HOUSE

INTRODUCTION:

COUNTRY HOUSE OR

HOUSE IN THE COUNTRY?

This book originated in a hotel lounge on the Kärntner Ring in the heart of Vienna. Gathered there with a group of European and American friends following an exhausting tour of Schönbrunn Palace, I found myself struggling to define and defend the expression "an *American* country house." Then — and subsequently as I worked on this book — I learned that anyone who mentions or proposes to write a book on American country houses will immediately be challenged: What do you mean by a country house? And what houses will be included? One's reply to these questions will inevitably disappoint or even anger the questioner, because country houses — however ill defined — evoke a more emotional response among Americans than any other form of architecture. "Surely you'll include . . . ," followed by the name of a favored property, is the usual reaction. The more knowledgeable the questioner, the more obscure the house will be, and the more vociferous the objection at its omission.

Most Americans understand, even if they are never called upon to articulate, the difference between a "country house" and a "house in the country." The latter phrase usually refers to a farm house or a more or less secluded vacation retreat. If occupied year round, it may be called a "country home" and will come complete with casual furniture and the aroma of baking apple pies.

The term "country house" is laden with Anglo-Irish cultural overtones that imply a structure of architectural distinction — if not pretension — associated with a landed estate and enhanced by the patina of age. It also helps if the house and the surrounding garden have been in the embellishing hands of the same family for several generations.

One of my companions that fateful day in Vienna, an authority on famous English country houses, stated flatly that there was no American tradition of country houses and certainly no "type" that could be called typical. He even went so far as to quote the late Vita Sackville-West (in a little book entitled *English Country Houses*, I later learned) to the effect that "there is nothing quite like the English country house anywhere else in the world. France has her chateaux, Italy her historic villas, Spain her gardens . . . , Germany her robber castles, but the exact equivalent of what we mean by the English country house is not to be found elsewhere."

Of course Sackville-West was speaking romantically and as an Englishwoman raised at Knole who created the famous country house garden at Sissinghurst — rather than as an architectural historian. In addition to the monumental ducal structures like Knole, Chatsworth, and Blenheim, she had in mind houses of any size and material that share an indefinable "knack of fitting in" to the countryside and probably include — in addition to the house itself — a mix of field dogs and Wellington boots, a garden containing phlox and old roses, and chintz slipcovers over inherited furniture.

You don't have to be an architectural historian to visualize an English country house. But the American country house is not so easily circumscribed. It has had a shorter time in which to develop; yet, being the product of a large and varied continent that enjoys a greater ethnic diversity, its tradition is more complex and exciting. During many of the centuries in which celebrated English country houses were being erected, America was just beginning to be settled. Architecture begins only when the environment is under control, when resources can be spared to erect dwellings that meet psychological needs rather than those of basic shelter. Formal architecture also requires a mature society. Only then do builders and

architects who make their living exclusively from designing and supervising the construction of buildings emerge.

The first recognizable group of American country houses begins to appear as a product of the plantation culture of Maryland, Virginia, North Carolina, and South Carolina in the early years of the eighteenth century, as large tracts of agricultural land began to be concentrated in the hands of a few wealthy and politically powerful families. Like the great country houses of England, which were symbolic expressions of the wealth and power derived from the ownership of the land, these houses were agriculturally based. In the greater sweep of Western history, these houses must be judged something of an anachronism, for the age of agricultural estates as the basis of wealth and power was already on the wane in Britain; across the Midlands could be heard the sibilance of steam and the ceaseless clack of looms. But in America, slavery perpetuated an agricultural system that encouraged the construction of great country houses, and would continue to do so until the mid-nineteenth century.

These southern plantation houses, developed in the century and a half that European-Americans were confined to a narrow band of settlement along the Atlantic coastline, are perhaps the only American country houses that closely resemble their English counterparts, the land-based family seats. After the Revolution, as Americans traveled west in large numbers for the first time, they did not always take the tradition of the great plantation house with them.

The vastness of the American frontier, in Robert Frost's words, the land ". . . vaguely realizing westward, But still unstoried, artless, unenhanced . . . ," encouraged a century of rootlessness — a rootlessness that is fatal to settled architecture. The distinctly American failure to develop more than a general pride of place, coupled with a disregard for the long-range environmental and visual consequences of building for the moment and then moving on, contributes to the scarcity of architecturally significant country houses in America.

While most of the settlers drawn to the frontier would be classified as farmers who never owned more than a few hundred acres with a simple farm house, there were speculators and landowners with large holdings who erected country houses intended to be visible evidence of their owners' wealth and power. This was especially true where slave ownership encouraged labor-intensive, single-crop plantations. But the elimination of the principles of primogenitor (whereby an estate passed by right of inheritance to the first-born son) and entail (limiting inheritance to a specified line of heirs) encouraged the division of large agricultural holdings. As a consequence, the number of estates that continue after two or three hundred years to be the "seats" of important families in America can practically be numbered on the fingers of two hands.

The Country Seats of the United States of North America,

with some Scenes connected with them.

PART the FIRST

Containing Twenty Plates.

The View from Springland.

Designed and Published 1808, by W. Birch Enamel Painter Springland near Bristol Pennsyl.a

The artist William Birch (1755–1834) migrated in 1794 from his native England to Philadelphia where he published The Country Seats of the United States of North America *in 1808, the first illustrated book on American country houses and villas. "The comforts and advantages of a Country Residence," Birch wrote, ". . . consist more in the beauty of the situation, than in the massy magnitude of the edifice. . . . The man of taste will select his situation with skill, and add elegance and animation to the best choice. In the United States the face of nature is so variegated . . . , and the means so easy of acquiring positions fit to gratify the most refined and rural enjoyment, that labour and expenditure of Art is not so great as in Countries less favoured." (*The Athenaeum of Philadelphia*)

One of the "country seats" recorded by William Birch is Hampton near Baltimore, Maryland, principal residence of the Ridgely family for six generations and one of the most important American country houses to survive from the Federal period. Erected by the mariner, planter, and iron master Charles Ridgely (1733–1790) beginning in 1783, Hampton commanded an empire of 24,000 slave-cultivated acres and a highly successful ironworks. Ridgely's nephew, Charles Carnan Ridgely, further enhanced the family fortunes and served three terms as governor of Maryland. (The Athenaeum of Philadelphia)

Yet along the seaboard, a different sort of country house, which in the eighteenth and early nineteenth centuries would have been called a villa, had emerged. Villas began to appear in the eighteenth century in the environs of the new cities of the North, where merchants and manufacturers gathered to be near the source of their wealth. Quite different from the great English country house and tracing its origins to houses erected along the Thames River near London, the "villa" was, in the eighteenth century, a seasonal country dwelling of smallish, symmetrical, and classical character located within a comfortable day's journey by boat, coach, or horse from Philadelphia, New York, Boston, and Baltimore.

The fortunes of the Ridgely family and of Hampton steadily declined in the second half of the nineteenth and the first half of the twentieth century, largely as a consequence of repeated divisions of the estate as it passed from generation to generation. In the 1930s the owners were reduced to selling suburban building lots, family portraits, and the famous Hampton wine cellar. In 1948 the house and a few acres were acquired by the National Park Service and opened to the public as a museum. (Historic Hampton, Inc.)

Often with pleasure gardens attached, villas were *in* the country without being *of* the country. Typically they did not adjoin income-producing lands but reflected economic, social, and political success achieved elsewhere. As residences they were to provide a pleasant retreat from the heat and odors of the city, or an escape from the yellow fever, typhoid, and cholera that regularly savaged urban populations. While often classed as country houses, the classical villas of the eighteenth and early nineteenth centuries served an entirely different role in the lives of their owners, and they functioned much differently as residences.

The generally accepted definition of what constitutes a villa in America began to change in the 1830s and 1840s, in part as a consequence of the influence of the Scottish landscape-gardener and architectural critic John Claudius Loudon on the New York architect Alexander Jackson Davis and the Hudson River Valley horticulturist and architectural critic Andrew Jackson Downing. Loudon described a villa as a residence in the country with a garden for "recreation and enjoyment, more than profit." Unlike the classical villa, however, Loudon's villas could be located away from a city and might be occupied year round as the principal residence of a family.

According to Davis and Downing—whose fruitful collaboration in the 1840s gave America some of its most appealing examples of the romantic villa in the Hudson River Valley—such houses should be picturesque so they would, in Loudon's words, "exercise some influence on the imagination; and therefore . . . be accompanied, as far as practicable, by such circumstances as may service to heighten its effect on the mind."

Through Downing's many publications, particularly *The Architecture of Country Houses* (1850) and his earlier *Cottage Residences* (1842), he advanced the case for several variations of the romantic Gothic Revival and Italianate Revival styles. "The villa—the country house," he writes, "should, above all things, manifest individuality. It should say something of the character of the family within—as much as possible of their life and history, their tastes and associations, should mould and fashion themselves upon its walls." Downing continues, "what we mean by a villa, in the United States, is the country house of a person of competence or wealth sufficient to build and maintain it with some taste and elegance." Unlike the farm house or cottage—the latter defined "as a dwelling so small that the household duties may all be performed by the family, or with the assistance of not more than one or two domestics"—the villa is a "country house of larger accommodations, requiring the care of at least three or more servants."

By illustrating villas in a variety of styles, Downing helped to create a demand for such houses throughout the country that architects and pattern-book publishers rushed to supply. It is fairly safe to say that any region of the continental United States where settlers were not outnumbered by Native Americans, long-horn cows, or free-ranging buffalo can boast of Downing-inspired villas built to demonstrate the owner's "taste and elegance."

The villa—closely tied to urban transportation and manufacturing in the North—and the plantation country house—seat of agrarian wealth and power—developed on parallel tracks until the Civil War brought an end to the plantation house. But this did not bring country house building to an end. In the late nineteenth and early twentieth centuries, industrialists, railroad magnates, stock manipulators, actors, and assorted entrepreneurs from all walks of life—many of whom had grown wealthy in the war that humbled the South—converted their enormous incomes into great piles of masonry that they often called—without intentional irony—"country houses."

These houses represent the ultimate consumption of

wealth derived from means other than the land. Most were set pieces, splendid suburban palaces near major metropolitan areas or seasonal watering holes. Their size and extravagance notwithstanding, the seaside "cottages" of Newport, Rhode Island, the summer places of Southampton, Long Island, and the winter retreats along the golden beaches of Florida and California are not truly country houses, even if the ideal of country house life helped to motivate their construction.

But for those few with the means to express a romantic fascination with the *idea* of the country house, who insisted on carrying their admiration — some might say envy — of the ducal estates of England and the chateaux of France to the ultimate extreme, and for whom the ownership of a fifty-room establishment on a modest suburban tract of a few acres could never be enough, the vast expanse of North America offered opportunity. The ultimate expressions of this megalomania are achieved by George Washington Vanderbilt at Biltmore and William Randolph Hearst at San Simeon — the last great country houses of America, on tracts to rival the landed estates of pre-industrial Europe when an owner measured his wealth in acres, crops, and serfs who could be called to arms.

Sitting in that Vienna hotel, I finally had to agree with Vita Sackville-West, there is nothing quite like the English country house in America. But that is what makes American country houses so fascinating — they are not homogeneous nor all variations on one theme. I thought to trace their path across the country and across time, from the southern plantations of tidewater Virginia and Maryland to the palaces overlooking the Pacific, would make a compelling journey that might reveal much about our national character and aspirations.

1

THE AMERICAN COUNTRY

HOUSE AND VILLA

America's most famous country houses are myth. The image is burned indelibly in the American subconscious: Gerald O'Hara and his daughter Scarlett etched starkly against a blood-red sky. In the background — Tara, a modest, whitewashed brick house with four square pillars supporting a two-story shed roof extending from the eaves.

Down the road from the O'Haras live the wealthier, more educated and polished Wilkes family in their plantation house, Twelve Oaks: a Grecian pile with pedimented portico and wide verandas through which a visitor enters a vast hall with double-spiraling stairway, designed not merely to facilitate passage from one floor to another, but for dramatic entrances by beautifully clad young ladies whose coquettish glances belie their virginal demeanors. There is the scent of magnolia in the air, the soft clink of mule harness in the distance as the contented field hands return to their quarters . . . all is right in the world.

The houses of Margaret Mitchell's *Gone With the Wind*, like the "land of Cavaliers and Cotton Fields called the Old South," are "no more than a dream remembered."

Or are they?

Ignoring for the moment the countless Tara clones erected on American suburban developments during the past half century, it is possible to discover genuine houses throughout the Confederacy that readily evoke the novelist's and motion picture producer's nostalgic, soft-focus image of pre–Civil War plantation society, the stock in trade of hoop-skirted docents.

Regrettably, most of these plantation house museums are bereft of the lands that spawned and nurtured them, thereby throwing the greater emphasis upon the house

Stuccoed brick Houmas House (c. 1840), near Burnside, Louisiana, focal point of a large sugar plantation, survived the Civil War because its owner was a British subject. The house and its hexagonal garçonnières (outbuilding accommodations for the sons of the family) are so evocative that they have been used by Hollywood filmmakers, most notably for the haunting Bette Davis motion picture Hush . . . Hush Sweet Charlotte (1965). (Photograph by Jim Zietz)

and its contents. Scarlett's father reminds us of the essence of the land in the 1939 motion picture version of *Gone With the Wind*. When Scarlett protests that she cares nothing for Tara, her father remarks, "Why, the *land* is the only thing in the world worth working for, worth fighting for — worth dying for — because it's the only thing that lasts." While he gazes across fertile fields to the house as he utters these words, Gerald O'Hara knows that it is only a by-product of the land. Tara and Twelve Oaks—especially Twelve Oaks—are tangible symbols of the wealth and power the land confers. They are also the last country houses in America of a type that would have been understood by British-Americans of the seventeenth and eighteenth centuries.

From the Middle Ages until industrialization changed the economic balance of the modern nation-state, land was the fountainhead of wealth and power. Of course, both might be acquired by other means—service to the Crown or commerce, for example—but unsupported by land, such emoluments could prove transitory. Land provided wealth through cash crops, rents from the tenants who actually farmed, and, especially in the American colonies, speculation in undeveloped land itself.

In both England and the colonies, the ownership of land also conferred access to political power. The landowner with large holdings in Virginia might serve as a colonel of the militia, sheriff, or county court justice, and certainly he would be a parish vestryman or warden in the established church. As he became wealthier and forged links with other planter families through carefully selected marriages for himself and his children, he might be sent to the House of Burgesses and then appointed to the Governor's Council, which often led to other lucrative offices and certainly provided access to the undeveloped lands belonging to the government.

In seventeenth-century Virginia, large plantations were not typical; yeoman farmers usually owned tracts of twenty to five hundred acres, and white indentured servants provided most of the labor. By the turn of the century, however, black slaves began to be imported in large numbers, and slave labor made plantations profitable on a scale not previously possible. (On the eve of the Revolution, there were 750,000 blacks and 2,500,000 whites in the thirteen colonies.) As the number of slaves increased, free farmers found themselves gradually squeezed off the land; they opted to move west or north. New immigrants found coastal plantation colonies increasingly less attractive destinations. Edward Randolph explained in 1696 that members of the Virginia government "have from time to time procured grants of very large Tracts of land, so that there has not for many years been any waste land to be taken up by those who bring with them servants, or by such Servants, who have served their time faithfully with their Masters, but it is taken up and ingrossed beforehand."

By 1700 the great Virginia families, the Byrds, Carters, Fitzhughs, Lees, Randolphs, and others—in all fewer than a hundred families—had already begun intermarrying and consolidating land, wealth, and political control. A colonial aristocracy was emerging and would soon begin to erect country houses worthy of this new status and wealth; colonial houses to be sure, but created by and for British subjects who considered themselves as much a part of the imperial system as any county family in England. These were the first American country houses. As we will see in the next chapter, houses like Rosewell, Westover, Stratford, and Shirley did not appear until this new aristocracy had settled into power and began to generate sufficient disposable wealth to afford such grandeur, a condition encouraged by the steady rise in tobacco prices throughout the first half of the eighteenth century.

Typically, these land holdings were not contiguous; they might be widely scattered over several counties and range in size from a few hundred to many thousands of acres. (Robert "King" Carter owned 300,000 acres spread over several Virginia counties.) Normally, however, there would be a "home" or "manor" plantation that became the central administrative hub of the entire estate, and there the owner would erect his principal

One of the justly famous Virginia country houses is Carter's Grove near Williamsburg, erected for Carter Burwell (1716–1756) by master builder David Minetree, c.1750. In the 1920s the house was acquired by Mr. and Mrs. Archibald McCrea, who changed the roofline and added hyphens to connect the flanking buildings to the main block of the house. (Colonial Williamsburg Foundation)

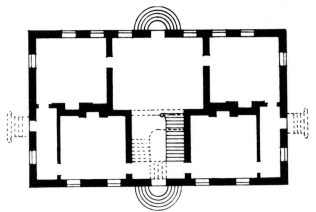

Ground-floor plan of Carter's Grove.

An idea of how Carter's Grove appeared prior to the McCrea alterations is conveyed in this photograph by Edward Beckwith (c.1926). The front porch was a nineteenth-century addition. (Colonial Williamsburg Foundation)

residence. English historian Mark Girouard offers a description of country houses that might equally well be applied to the larger estates of mid-eighteenth-century tidewater:

Land provided the fuel, a country house was the engine which made it effective. It achieved this in a number of ways. It was the headquarters from which land was administered and power organised. It was a show-case, in which to exhibit and entertain supporters and good connections. . . . It was an image-maker, which projected an aura of glamour, mystery or success around its owner. It was visible evidence of his wealth. It showed his credentials — even if the

The entrance hall and stair of Carter's Grove are the work of Richard Baylis, an English joiner brought to Virginia in 1751 to finish the interior. (Colonial Williamsburg Foundation)

credentials were sometimes faked. Trophies in the hall, coats of arms over the chimney-pieces, books in the library and temples in the park could suggest that he was discriminating, intelligent, bred to rule and brave.

Unlike the wealthy planters of the sugar islands — who expected to return to England laden with imperial booty to embellish the countryside of Kent or Sussex, and thus tended not to translate the wealth they derived from the land into monumental New World country houses — the planters of Maryland, Virginia, and the Carolinas put down roots, erected appropriate seats for their families, and considered themselves members of His Majesty's empire living permanently in one of his richest and most loyal colonies.

Because the rivers provided easy access to the outside world, the South did not develop large cities in the colonial period. Nor were they needed. The Rev. Hugh Jones remarked in 1724, "any Thing may be delivered to a Gentleman there from London, Bristol &c. with less Trouble and Cost, than to one living five Miles in the Country in England . . . ," and according to Sir John Oldmixon, who visited Maryland and Virginia, this advantage "hinders the Increase of Towns; indeed every Plantation is a little Town of itself, and can subsist itself with Provisions and Necessaries, every considerable Planter's Warehouse being like a Shope. . . ." Of course, those planters whose plantations suffered hostile climates, such as Middleton Place and Drayton Hall on the Ashley River near Charleston, South Carolina, might also construct town houses in settlements such as Charleston and Savannah.

From his landing, the colonial plantation owner looked to London, Bristol, Liverpool, or Glasgow as his metropolis, not to Annapolis, Williamsburg, or Charles-

Drayton Hall (1738–42) is one of the most important Ashley River plantations to survive both the Revolution and the Civil War. The two-story portico is based on Andrea Palladio's Villa Pisani (1555). (National Trust for Historic Preservation, photograph by Grayson Mathews)

ton. He consigned cash crops such as tobacco, rice, and indigo to a world market through his British factor and received by return ship the latest fashions in architecture, dress, and furnishings for his household — unlike those in the North who increasingly received their goods and services from the cities of Philadelphia, New York, Newport, and Boston. In 1755 the Potomac River planter George Washington ordered from London "a Mahogany bedstead with carved and fluted pillars . . . six mahogany chairs with gothic arched backs . . . a fine neat, mahogany serpentine dressing table with mirrors and brass trimmings. . . ." That same year his near neighbor, George Mason, not content with obtaining architecture from books, had his younger brother in London engage a promising carpenter and joiner trained in the latest fash-

ion. Young William Buckland agreed to a four-year indenture, and Gunston Hall, one of the most splendidly embellished American country houses, is the result. In Virginia alone the "Golden Age" of 1725–75 produced Berkeley, Rosewell, Westover, Stratford, Sabine Hall, Mount Vernon, Shirley, Mount Airy, Wilton, Carter's Grove, Blandfield, Kenmore, Gunston Hall, Montpelier,

The Joseph Manigault House (c.1803), Charleston, South Carolina, was designed by Gabriel Manigault for his rice-planter brother, one of the wealthiest men in the state. (Charleston Museum)

and the first Monticello—to name just the obvious examples among those houses that survive. In the next chapter we will take a closer look at several of these houses and the families that built them.

When the plantation system appeared in the North during the colonial era, it rarely produced country houses of more than regional significance. Usually in the local or vernacular style, those northern country houses would more appropriately be called farm houses. Harriton, for example, a plantation house in Pennsylvania, was originally built by the Welsh Quaker Rowland Ellis. In 1682, Ellis received a grant of seven hundred acres from William Penn a few miles from newly surveyed Philadelphia in what is now the prosperous suburb of Bryn Mawr, a name taken from the one originally chosen by Ellis for his new, two-story stone house. Bryn Mawr was erected in 1704 to replace the rude log cabin that had been built to shelter the farmer sent to prepare the land for cultivation.

In the best colonial tradition, Ellis attempted to profit as speculator rather than farmer and ran into financial difficulty. In 1719 he sold Bryn Mawr to Richard Har-

Gunston Hall (1755–59), Fairfax County, Virginia, was the home of the revolutionary George Mason, father of the Bill of Rights. Deceptive in scale and understated on the exterior, the house boasts interior woodwork that ranks with the finest carving in colonial America. (HABS, photograph by Jack E. Boucher)

rison, a Maryland planter from the Western Shore of the Chesapeake, who renamed the house Harriton and moved his family and slaves to Pennsylvania, where he raised tobacco on the surrounding fields. The house eventually came into the hands of Harrison's daughter, who married Charles Thomson, the leading revolutionary of Philadelphia, who was to become secretary of the Continental Congress. After Thomson's death, Harriton was occupied by tenant farmers until it became the suburban home of a prosperous local architect in the late 1920s.

Architecturally, Harriton is a better-than-average vernacular stone farm house of the type erected in the thousands by greater or lesser landholders in southeastern Pennsylvania in the colonial and early national period. This type would be replicated across the country as the ever-restless Scotch-Irish moved westward after

The center passage of Gunston Hall suggests the richness of William Buckland's woodwork. This space has recently been reinterpreted; the wallpaper reproduces a mid-eighteenth-century document found in the collections of the Victoria & Albert Museum, London. (Board of Regents, National Society of Colonial Dames of America, photograph by Dennis McWaters)

Blandfield is one of the less famous examples of British Palladian planta-tion houses of mid-eighteenth-century Virginia that may have been based on plates intended for Vitruvius Scoticus (Edinburgh, 1750). Erected by William Beverley (1696–1756) and named for his wife, Elizabeth Bland Beverley, the 3,500-acre working plantation remained in the family for ten generations. (Photograph by Willie Graham)

the Revolution. Harriton's particular claim to fame, and principal justification for being a house museum, is its association with the now little-known Charles Thomson, whom John Adams called "The Sam Adams of Phila-delphia, the life of the cause of liberty."

The Harrisons' brief effort to introduce tobacco cul-tivated by slave labor into Pennsylvania is an exception to the general rule, and in areas north of the Mason-Dixon Line there are few successful examples of the

Harriton [originally called Bryn Mawr] was erected near Philadelphia in 1704 by Quaker Rowland Ellis, who named it for his home in Wales. From 1719 to 1759 the slave-owning Harrison family raised tobacco there, one of the northernmost documented examples of the plantation system in America. (Photograph by George Vaux, ARPS)

plantation system in the colonial period. The Livingston, Wadsworth, and Clarke families in New York, for example, had vast, nearly feudal estates that conferred on their holders wealth and political power derived mainly from tenants' rents and land speculation. But in the eigh-teenth century, these estates tended not to be focused on a single power center, and probably because of their close proximity to New York City (and eventually its satellite, Albany), the need for the year-round country house as administrative center was not pressing.

Hyde Hall, near Cooperstown, New York, was the country house of George Hyde Clarke, who inherited title to more than 100,000 acres that were leased to tenant farmers. Designed by the Albany architect Philip Hooker, the house was under construction from 1817 to 1835 and remained in Clarke family hands until 1963. (Photograph by Milo Stewart)

Hyde Hall provides the backdrop for the wedding of Anne Hyde Clarke to Arthur Osgood Choate on October 16, 1907. (New York State Historical Association)

From virtually the earliest days of settlement, the smaller and less populated northern colonies had developed urban centers of trade and, later, manufacturing. Concurrently, a pattern of rural land use evolved that favored smaller family farms that never were supplanted by large, single-crop, slave-cultivated agricultural estates. While the grandees of northern trade and commerce might own and speculate in vast tracts of undeveloped land, they lived by necessity in the cities, close to the true source of their wealth and the centers of colonial government. Mostly British-born, bred to favor country living and to measure success in terms of symbolic country seats, they embraced the classical villa as an acceptable compromise.

Because these eighteenth- and early-nineteenth-century American villas were by definition within easy reach of cities that have now expanded beyond all recognition, country houses of the villa type have largely been lost. (Even the term, once commonly used, is rarely understood today except by architectural historians.) Isolated examples survive in or near modern Baltimore, New York, and Boston, but the finest group of surviving villas is to be found in Philadelphia, due to the happy circumstance of the largest urban park in the world having been developed along the banks of the Schuylkill River in the mid-nineteenth century. As a consequence, Chapter 3 will examine the Philadelphia villas in some depth.

Whether southern planters or northern merchants, colonial Americans agreed upon the desirability of access

Gracie Mansion, now the official residence of the mayor of New York City, was erected by the Scot shipping magnate Archibald Gracie (1755–1829) in 1799 and enlarged between 1802 and 1808. Josiah Quincy described Gracie's villa as "upon the East River, opposite the famous pass called Hell Gate. The scene is beautiful beyond description. A deep, broad, rapid stream glances with an arrowy fleetness by the shore, hurrying along every species of vessel which the extensive commerce of the country affords." (The Gracie Mansion Conservancy)

to the West. Unfortunately, more than the Appalachian Mountains stood in the way. Crown efforts to conciliate the Indians had resulted in a proclamation that forbade colonial governors to grant lands "beyond the heads or Sources of any of the Rivers which fall into the Atlantic Ocean. . . ." Settlement on Indian lands west of the Appalachians was forbidden — settlers already there were ordered to return — and it became illegal to purchase Indian land.

The Revolution removed these restrictions on westward migration. Soon after the war, the states ceded to the new national government most of their western claims. Now the trapper and trader, the speculator and settler were free to exploit the public domain largely unhampered by the distant, weak government whose surveyors, land agents, governors, and judges often arrived long after the early stages of settlement. The pent-up demand for land — particularly from southern farm fam-

ilies who increasingly suffered from a combination of wasteful, unscientific agriculture and the consolidation of land in the hands of wealthy slave-owners—propelled Americans through the mountain passes and across the continent. Such colorful figures as Daniel Boone and John Donelson, whose party of thirty frontier families settled on a bend of the Cumberland River in 1780 at a

One of the few classical villas to survive in the Boston area is Gore Place (1806) at Waltham, a short journey up the Charles River. Christopher Gore planned his house with Jacques-Guillaume Legrand (1743–1807), which may help to explain its sophistication. Gore became governor of Massachusetts in 1809. (Photograph by Richard Cheek)

place they named Fort Nashborough (later Nashville), led Americans westward. Kentucky (1792) and Tennessee (1796) became states within a few years of the British defeat at Yorktown, quickly followed by Ohio (1803), Indiana (1816), and Illinois (1818). One British traveler observed, "Old America seems to be breaking up, and moving westward."

New Englanders moving into central New York, northern Ohio, Michigan, and subsequently into the upper Midwest, tended to be small holders seeking rich bottom land to replace their granite-ledge farms. Assisted by their children and a few hired hands, they tilled the land and erected vernacular farm houses that would give the region its New England architectural flavor. The Wadsworth family was an exception.

Jeremiah Wadsworth of Hartford, Connecticut, who had been commissary general of the Continental army,

acquired 200,000 acres of Genesee River Valley land in western New York and dispatched his two nephews, James and William Wadsworth, to act as agents. Once on the site, the brothers began to acquire land for themselves, ultimately securing title to some 70,000 acres that they intended to sell. Unfortunately, this proved difficult because many settlers could not afford or hadn't the credit to purchase land, even at relatively low prices. The Wadsworths consequently retained title and leased their land on a variety of terms (annual renewal became common by the 1830s); in this way the fields were cleared, houses erected, taxes paid, and the owners provided with income. This leasehold tenancy continues to this day; many of the families tilling Wadsworth land have been there for generations.

The Wadsworth holdings have contributed to the preservation of open, unspoiled farm land that makes the Genesee Valley so attractive. They have also made it possible for the Wadsworths to live an English country life-style of the sort that is more often spoken of than realized in North America. In 1835, the Wadsworths erected a country house to replace their modest New England, Greek Revival farm house. Hartford House was inspired — so the family believes — by a London town house the Wadsworths had seen while on their wedding trip. The product of successive alterations, Hartford House today consists of a three-bay, three-story, stuccoed central block and two flanking pavilions connected by hyphens. Despite the single-story, classical revival *porte-cochère* (carriage entrance), its unadorned late-Georgian origins are still apparent. To this day Hartford House remains the seat of the Wadsworth family and home of the Genesee Valley Hunt founded by W. Austin Wadsworth in 1876.

Settlers moving west in the post-Revolution period from Maryland, Virginia, and the Carolinas into Kentucky, Tennessee, northern Georgia, and Alabama brought with them the plantation system that would — once the initial period of raw settlement had passed — produce some of the most notable American country houses. The rivers that drained this vast watershed became the grasping fingers of settlement reaching into the tributaries of the Ohio and Mississippi. At each juncture new settlements formed or developed around earlier trading posts — Marietta, Portsmouth, Cincinnati, Louisville, and so on. Cash crops from western Virginia, Ohio, Tennessee, and Kentucky went upriver to Pittsburgh or down the Ohio and Mississippi, where they joined the offerings of Missouri, Arkansas, and the Deep South on their way to New Orleans and world markets beyond. Navigable waterways played a seminal role in the history of American country houses in all parts of the country,

During their wedding trip to England in 1834, Mr. and Mrs. James S. Wadsworth admired the house in Regent's Park designed by Decimus Burton (1800–1881) for the third marquis of Hertford (built in 1825, demolished in 1937) that inspired what came to be known as Hartford House in the Genesee Valley of New York. (Photograph by Daniel Fink)

The Genesee Valley Hunt, founded by W. Austin Wadsworth in 1876, is one of the oldest and most famous fox hunts in the United States. Eschewing traditional (British!) pinks in favor of the blue and buff of the Revolutionary American army, the opening-day field typically exceeds one hundred riders. (Photograph by Daniel Fink)

but nowhere is this more obvious than in the South prior to the coming of the transportation revolution. In the nineteenth century the railroad would be the genesis and explain the importance of such inland cities as Atlanta, Georgia, just as the canal system had earlier linked the Great Lakes Basin to the Eastern Seaboard, especially to New York City.

The rich land of the territory northwest of the Ohio River (the present states of Ohio, Indiana, Illinois, Michigan, Wisconsin) became available for settlement after General Anthony Wayne disposed of Indian claims to lands that the new United States intended to use to reward veterans of the late war with Great Britain. One of many enterprising Virginians drawn by the opening of Ohio was Thomas Worthington (1773–1827), a young man of modest estate who first came to the territory to locate and survey land for others near what eventually

became Chillicothe. Realizing at once the opportunity at hand, he had by 1798 purchased military warrants to 5,000 acres, hired a gang of manumitted slaves (slavery having been banned in the territory by the Ordinance of 1787), and relocated himself and his bride. In the new community, he became a major figure: justice of the peace, colonel of the militia, and judge of the court of common pleas. Ultimately he would own over 25,000 acres, and by the end of his life he had been a member of the territorial legislature, the Ohio Constitutional Convention, and the Ohio House of Representatives, a United States senator, and governor of the state.

Most transplanted Virginians, like their New England and Pennsylvania counterparts moving on parallel tracks to the north, erected vernacular farm houses that differed little from what their great-grandfathers had built a century before. Thomas Worthington, however, aspired to something equal to his station. While in Washington, D.C., representing the new state of Ohio, he met Benjamin Henry Latrobe (1764–1820)—America's first professional architect. From designs by Latrobe, in 1806 Worthington began a new house of native sandstone that he would eventually name Adena, "signifying (in the Hebrew language) pleasure," Worthington recorded in his diary. We know the house was nearly completed by the following year because Fortescue Cuming reports in his *Sketches of a Tour to the Western Country* (1810) that on August 14, 1807, he "walked before breakfast half a mile through the woods to the northward, to an elegant seat belonging to Col. Worthington. It will be finished in a few weeks and will be one of the best and most tasty [i.e., tasteful] houses not only of this state, but to the westward of the Allegheny mountains. It is about sixty feet square, with a square roof, and two large receding wings. . . . it is built with freestone, but the stone of the front is all hewn and squared, like the generality of the houses in the new part of Glasgow in Scotland, the stone being very similar both in colour and quality."

For all his political activity, Worthington operated the home farm himself; other farms he rented out for a percentage of the crops or hired overseers to manage. His records show he raised corn, wheat, rye, oats; clover and timothy for hay; flax, hemp, and fruit. Adena also enjoyed contracts to supply pork and lard to the military; in addition, Worthington kept a large herd of cattle and introduced Merino sheep. What was not consumed locally went downriver to New Orleans.

The year before Worthington died, Karl Bernhard, duke of Saxe-Weimar Eisenach, stayed overnight at Adena, described as Worthington's "country-seat two miles from Chillicothe, where he enjoys his rents and the revenue of his considerable property." Writing in his *Travels Through North America* (1828), Bernard tells us:

Thomas Worthington hired two Virginia stonemasons and a Pennsylvania carpenter named Conrad Christman to execute Benjamin Henry Latrobe's design for a country house near Chillicothe, Ohio, 1806–1807. He named it Adena. (Ohio Historical Society)

"The governor's house is . . . very commodious, the furniture plain, but testifies the good taste and easy circumstances of the owner." While not equal to the mansions of tidewater erected in the golden age of the mid-eighteenth century, Adena is nonetheless recognizable as a country house of the plantation type: designed to reflect the wealth and power of an owner who initially derived both from the land.

During the Federal period (1790s–1820s), many farm houses tracing their architectural origins to the formal, more academically self-conscious country houses of the East were erected in Ohio, Kentucky, and Tennessee by prosperous farmers, some of whom (south of the Ohio River) owned slaves and planted tobacco. Welcome Hall in Woodford County, Kentucky, is a particularly good example. William Lee Graddy had emigrated from North Carolina in 1787 to the Kentucky bluegrass region, where he purchased an existing two-story house of local lime-

stone with end chimneys, steep roof, and one wing. The Graddys added another wing, which created a balanced composition, and a two-story porch, c.1828. Like Harriton of the previous century, Welcome Hall is a particularly appealing representative of a regional farm-house type that probably should not be called a country house. It is nonetheless a rare survival. The house remains to this day in the Graddy family and is largely unchanged; most of the interior woodwork in the local vernacular is as it was when installed, and most of the original outbuildings near the house survive.

Similar examples of unpretentious houses of architectural importance that remain in family hands do exist throughout America; these are largely unsung because

One of the most appealing and yet comparatively modest late-Federal farm houses in the bluegrass region of Kentucky is Welcome Hall, erected in 1798, with additions, including the two-story pedimented porch, c.1828. This rare survival, with its interior woodwork and outbuildings largely intact, has remained in the Graddy family for over 150 years. (Photograph by Patricia S. DeCamp)

the families are principally of local stature and the houses rarely seen in national publications. Like Welcome Hall in Kentucky, Borough House in Stateburg, Sumter County, South Carolina, which has been owned and occupied by the Anderson family since the early nineteenth century and is now operated as a tree plantation, should be better known.

Stateburg is in the healthful upland plateau area of South Carolina settled in the eighteenth century. The original portion of the house was erected in 1758, and during the Revolution it served as British General Cornwallis's headquarters for a time and was then seized by the American army under General Greene. (At this time the house belonged to Thomas Hooper, brother of William, a signer of the Declaration of Independence.)

Shortly after the War of 1812, Borough House was acquired by Dr. and Mrs. William Anderson, who added the wings and the two-tiered piazza with unfluted Ionic columns in 1821. Their sons, Confederate General Richard Anderson and the noted surgeon Dr. William W. Anderson (the younger), were both born on the plantation, and Dr. Anderson's office (a Greek Revival temple with Ionic columns) is but one of the several outbuildings that have survived.

The great country houses erected west of the Alleghenies in the early nineteenth century were virtually all a product of the single-crop plantation system. Another North Carolinian who crossed the mountains into the fertile valleys of Kentucky and Tennessee was William Polk, who secured appointment as surveyor-general of the Middle District of Tennessee in 1784. Polk speculated in land on his own behalf and eventually owned several thousand acres. On one tract of 5,648 acres west of Columbia, Tennessee, four of Polk's sons built country houses: Hamilton Place, Westwood, Ashwood, and Rattle and Snap—the latter built for George Polk, c.1850–55. Rattle and Snap stands today as one of the premier examples of the Greek Revival style in the United States, as does its contemporary, Belle Meade (1853–54), near Nashville, Tennessee, erected on 5,300 acres by William

Giles Harding, son of the first owner, John Harding, who purchased the plantation in 1807.

As the slave-cultivated regions of the United States entered a period of unprecedented prosperity in the 1840s and 1850s, the first significant number of substantial country houses erected in America since before the Revolution began to appear. The agrarian regions of America had just begun to enjoy the fruits of expansionism, a period of unchecked growth that ended abruptly with the depression of 1837, from which neither the mercantile

*A*mong the monumental and often lavish country houses erected in the border states during the two decades of prosperity before the Civil War is Rattle and Snap (c. 1850–55) near Columbia, Tennessee. The name is said to derive from the gambling game in which William Polk won the land from the governor of North Carolina. The handsomely restored house remains in private hands. (HABS photograph)

North nor the agrarian South would recover for several years. Not until the end of the 1840s did cotton prices recover, creating a period in the 1850s when profits soared. This prosperity, which was generally reflected in the sugar-growing areas of Louisiana as well, resulted in a period of country house building the likes of which had not been seen since the golden age of colonial Maryland, Virginia, and the Carolinas.

Like the Georgian country houses of eighteenth-century tidewater, the Greek Revival plantations of the an-

Now administered by the Association for the Preservation of Tennessee Antiquities, Belle Meade (1853–54 and later additions), near Nashville, is one of a group of fine Greek Revival houses erected in the region in the early 1850s. (Belle Meade Mansion, photograph by Susan E. Thomas/JT Publications, Inc.)

tebellum South were visible evidence of the wealth and power made possible by high profits from labor-intensive, single-crop agriculture based on enslaved labor. These

San Francisco Plantation, the house that sugar built, is itself a confection sitting directly on the Mississippi levee near Reserve, Louisiana. (Photograph by Jim Zietz)

Greek Revival country houses reflect a growing confidence and the hope (if not reality) of economic independence, which strengthened regionalism and made it *thinkable* to dissolve the Federal union.

Not all revolutions begin with bread riots. Some are made in times of relative prosperity by the leaders of society who are emboldened to think of changing the political order by the success of a social, economic, or political system that they fear might be threatened. Certainly the planters who supported revolution in the 1770s had just enjoyed a period of unprecedented prosperity that is reflected in the construction of the most important

The decorative painting of the interior woodwork, walls, and ceilings of San Francisco is an unusual survival that has been recently restored to its 1850s splendor. (Photograph by Jim Zietz)

Not all plantation houses were in the Greek Revival style. Rose Hill in Beaufort County, South Carolina, shows the asymmetrical composition, picturesque roofline, and lancet arches typical of a vertical board-and-batten Gothic Revival house. It was erected by Dr. John Kirk, a wealthy planter and physician who owned 154 slaves. Construction was interrupted by the Civil War, and the house stood incomplete until 1946. It recently was substantially damaged by fire. (HABS, photograph by Jack E. Boucher)

American country houses of the colonial era. The colonies had enjoyed the protection and commercial benefits of membership in the expanding British Empire while being left administratively in control of their own affairs to a great extent. Confronted by a reasonable policy, albeit ineptly pursued, to extract a greater share of the costs of the wars with Britain's archenemy, France — whose North American colonies had been for generations a source of trouble on the frontier — Americans demanded, in the words of the Virginia Bill of Rights, "the enjoyment of life and liberty, with the means of acquiring and pos-

sessing property, and pursuing and obtaining happiness and safety" without — needless to say — the interference of His Majesty's government.

Events leading to the Civil War a century later are sometimes called the second American revolution. Like their great-grandfathers who precipitated the quarrel with George III, leaders of another plantation culture rebelled against the federation established in the 1780s by the thirteen states out of the ashes of the original confederation. With their economic and social system endangered by the now more populated and industrialized North, the southern states seceded from the Union.

This gouache-and-collage painting of St. John Plantation, St. Martin Parish, Louisiana, was executed by Adrien Persac (1823–1873) in 1861. Built by Alexandre Etienne de Clouet (1812–1890) as the center of a 5,000-acre sugar plantation, the Greek Revival house of c.1855 survives and the surrounding lands still produce sugar, but the brick sugar factory and other outbuildings captured by Persac are gone. (Anglo-American Art Museum, Louisiana State University, Baton Rouge. Gift of the Friends of the Museum and Mrs. Ben Hamilton in memory of her mother, Mrs. Tela Meier Hamilton)

The bloodiest war in American history followed — a war that effectively marks the end for architecturally significant country houses as symbols of wealth and power derived from agrarian estates.

Architecturally, the Greek Revival had been the style of choice for most American country houses and villas in the 1830s and 1840s. In regions where the plantation system flourished, the formality of the Greek Revival style appealed to what even the strongest apologist for slavery would call a conservative agrarian group — a group unlikely to embrace readily the exotic revival styles being introduced in the 1840s and 1850s. In Philadelphia and New York, however, architects whose patrons were more likely to call for town houses and suburban villas than monumental country houses had already begun to move away from the Greek Revival style for residential commissions. The depression that began in 1837 created a hiatus in building during which several architects went bankrupt for lack of work. By the time the American economy recovered in the early 1840s, architects such as Alexander Jackson Davis in New York and John Notman in Philadelphia had embraced the romantic revivals inspired by the medieval and renaissance architecture of Europe. This shift from the classical villa of the eighteenth and early nineteenth centuries to the romantic architectural styles of the second half of the nineteenth century will become apparent in Chapter 4.

First introduced in the Hudson River Valley, the debate over what constituted an appropriate architectural style for American country and suburban villas creatively

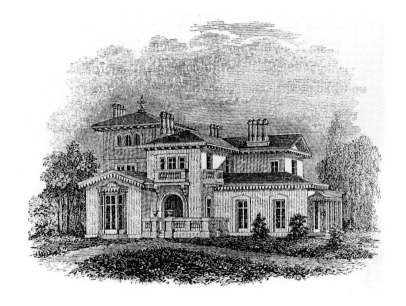

One of the first fully developed, picturesque Italianate villas in America was Riverside on the Delaware at Burlington, New Jersey, completed in 1839 to designs by John Notman (1810–1865) for the wealthy, ambitious Anglophile George Washington Doane, bishop of New Jersey. Downing published the design in his Treatise on the Theory and Practice of Landscape Gardening *(New York, 1841 and subsequent editions), and the Historic American Building Survey fortunately recorded the house before its demolition. (The Athenaeum of Philadelphia)*

launched Gothic, Italianate, Second Empire, and other revivals along waterways and near cities all across the country. A leisurely survey of Ohio and Mississippi riverbanks in the environs of cities such as Cincinnati and St. Louis reveals hundreds of architecturally distinguished and largely unsung mid- to late-nineteenth-century villas in various styles.

The rapid growth of American cities in the decades following the Civil War, and the development of greatly improved urban transportation, blurred the distinction between town and country. Large houses of architectural pretension erected on lots of more than a few acres —

houses that once might have been called villas, a term that gradually fell out of favor in the late nineteenth century — now were loosely called country houses, although the term eventually became associated in the popular press with Beaux-Arts classicism or chateauesque mansions erected in the late nineteenth and early twentieth centuries by wealthy industrialists, businessmen, and financiers. The final chapter will examine the most famous of these, one grandly in the style of French chateaux, the other a Spanish/Mexican pastiche that in its wonderful, if occasionally bizarre, amalgamation is happily and uniquely American.

2

THE FIRST AMERICAN

COUNTRY HOUSES

Our search for the American country house begins at the ruins of what may be the greatest of all. Rosewell — or what is left of it — stands in Gloucester County, Virginia, on the north bank of the York River approximately twenty-five miles by modern roads from the colonial capital at Williamsburg. All that remains are the looming pillars of the chimneys, now stabilized with steel and capped from the weather in a valiant effort to arrest the steady decay that has been Rosewell's fate for over 150 years. Photographs do not prepare the first-time visitor for the impact of Rosewell's rudely exposed bones. The house is shorn of an appropriate approach road, and the flanking dependencies that once created a forecourt and gave scale to the entire composition have disappeared. We are too close when the house comes into view, and we do not expect the height of what stands in the rough clearing. There is no other colonial structure built of this scale that is not a public building.

The comparison to a public building may be just what Mann Page, the builder of Rosewell, had in mind. His grandfather, who had arrived in Virginia by 1650, had prospered, as had his father Matthew Page (1659–1703), who became a county justice and a trustee of William and Mary College. Mann Page (1691–1730), the third generation of his family in Virginia, had been sent "home" to Eton and Oxford for a proper education.

As an aside, it should be said that, contrary to what many of us were taught in school, these tidewater planters were not the disinherited younger sons of English aristocrats. On the whole they came from relatively modest commercial backgrounds and made their way into the New World aristocracy by dint of hard work, a shrewd business sense, and a willingness to manage vast, often complex, business enterprises.

Their sons were generally trained in law, mathematics, and surveying — all skills needed to manage the business of a plantation — and were expected to deport themselves as English gentlemen, having been taught languages, philosophy, dancing, and music. This training, usually by tutors hired from England, the new college in Williamsburg, or the North, often drew on the well-stocked country house library. According to the diary of Philip Vickers Fithian, the young Princeton scholar who served as tutor at Nomini Hall — the manor house of Robert Carter III in Westmoreland County, Virginia — on the eve of the Revolution, that library (which he catalogued during his stay) consisted of over a thousand titles. And William Byrd II's library at Westover, one of the largest in America, was described as "consisting of near 4000 Volumes, in all Languages and Faculties, contained in twenty three double Presses of black walnut . . . the Whole in excellent Order. Great Part of the Books [are] in elegant Bindings, and of the best Editions, and a considerable Number of them very Scarce." After being tutored at home, the male children of plantation families typically were sent overseas for an education that might include time at the Inns of Court or enrollment at Oxford or Cambridge.

Shortly after Mann Page returned to Virginia, Governor Alexander Spotswood recommended him for his Council, calling him "a young gentleman of a liberal education, good parts, and a very plentiful estate, whose father and grandfather both had the honor of the same post." After his first wife died, Page married well. Judith Carter brought her new husband to the family circle of Robert "King" Carter of Corotoman (1663–1732), so called — according to Governor Francis Nicholson — not only for his wealth but for his "Pride & Ambition" and

*T*he ruins of Rosewell are all that remain of the greatest early-eighteenth-century American country house. It was erected by Mann Page (1691–1730) on the banks of the York River, c.1726. (Author's photograph)

*G*reen Spring, approximately four miles from Jamestown, was the most significant seventeenth-century plantation house in Virginia. Erected c.1650, it was for many years the home of Sir William Berkeley, governor of Virginia, and was described by his wife as "the finest seat in America & the only tolerable place for a Governour." Benjamin Henry Latrobe visited the house shortly after arriving in America in the 1790s and executed this watercolor. He confided to his diary that the owner intended "to pull down the present mansion and to erect a modest Gentleman's house near this spot. The antiquity of the old house . . . ought to plead in the project, but its inconvenience and deformity are more powerful advocates for its destruction. In it the oldest inhabited house in North America [sic] will disappear. . . ." Shortly thereafter the house was demolished. (Maryland Historical Society) ▶

his "haughtiness & insolence." As agent for Lord Fairfax's proprietorship on the Northern Neck of Virginia, Carter had an extraordinary opportunity to award to himself claims to tracts of undeveloped land; by his death he had amassed over 300,000 acres. In time-honored fashion, Carter cut his son-in-law in on this vast land grab, recording claims for Mann Page to 18,000 acres in one period of six years—giving him holdings of nearly 70,000 acres spread over nine counties.

Mann Page had inherited a modest wooden farm house that burned in 1721. Shortly thereafter he began to build Rosewell as visible evidence of his wealth and as an administrative center for his scattered plantations—a country house on a grander scale than anything here-

tofore seen in America. We unfortunately know little about King Carter's Corotoman, which may have inspired Page; it burned in the winter of 1729. Governor William Berkeley's Jacobean house at Green Spring, probably the largest seventeenth-century country house in the British mainland colonies, would have been considered greatly out of date by the 1720s. What Mann Page probably had his eye on was the new Governor's "Palace" in Williamsburg that had been authorized and begun in 1706. Both Rosewell and the Palace owe much to the blocky double-pile houses that began to appear in England in the mid-seventeenth century, the most famous of which was probably Coleshill, Berkshire (erected in 1650, burned in 1952), which, if not actually seen by Page when he was in England, would have been known to him and his anonymous master builder/architect through pattern books, some of which show similar detached pavilions forming a forecourt of service buildings for kitchen and stables and roof platforms with cupolas. There are so many possible sources that one historian of the Governor's Palace maintains that "we may be certain that the resemblance was due to collateral descent from common ancestors rather than to any more direct relationship."

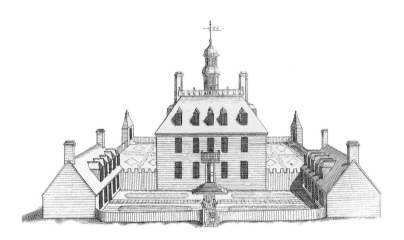

The famous Bodleian plate (a detail of the Governor's Palace is shown here) was discovered in the Rawlinson Collection at the Bodleian Library, Oxford, and was subsequently presented to Colonial Williamsburg. It probably was executed at the behest of William Byrd II to illustrate his History of the Dividing Line *and dates from the late 1730s. It became one of the chief documents for the Palace reconstruction. (Colonial Williamsburg Foundation)*

Construction of the Palace proved to be a prolonged affair; it was still a shell when Governor Spotswood arrived in 1710, intending to make Virginia his permanent home. Spotswood comes down to us as a sympathetic figure; Sir William Keith in his *History of the British Plantations in America* (London, 1738) says he "was well acquainted with Figures, and so good a Mathematician, that his skill in Architecture, and in the laying out of Ground to the best Advantage, is yet to be seen in Virginia, by the building of an elegant safe Magazine [for storing powder and arms], in the Centre of Williamsburgh, and in the considerable Improvements which he made to the Governor's House and Gardens." Spotswood pressured the Burgesses to authorize funds to complete the Palace, which was already well over budget, and laid out walls, garden, and gates that must have brought the complex close to that shown in the famous "Bodleian plate" on which the current reconstruction is largely based.

We can only speculate at Mann Page's motivations for planning a house larger than the Governor's Palace. At thirty Page was in his prime, and by all accounts he had the potential to become the leading citizen of Virginia. He had married the daughter and enjoyed the patronage of the wealthiest man in the colony, with whom he may have felt a need to compete; his wife had presented him with an heir and several extra male children to assure the continuation of his line; he sat as a member of the Governor's Council, which gave him powerful connections; and rising income from the sale of his tobacco promised even greater wealth. It was time for this Anglo-American planter to build a country house worthy of his position.

Photographs of Rosewell taken shortly before it was destroyed by fire in 1916 give some idea of the main block and permit a reasonably accurate reconstruction. The design owes much to Colen Campbell's *Vitruvius Britannicus*, whose volumes had appeared in 1715, 1717, and 1725 and helped to popularize neo-Palladian architecture in the American colonies. Unlike anything known to have been erected here previously, Rosewell was three full stories over a high basement. Its principal façades were five bays wide, with centrally placed doorways of cut stone and molded brick reached by imported Portland stone steps and platforms. The locally made bricks were laid in Flemish bond, and at the corners and around the window openings the brick was rubbed to provide additional visual interest. Some idea of the richness and skill with which this work was executed can be obtained from Christ Church; it was erected by Page's father-in-law in 1732 during the time Rosewell was being completed and may be by the same hand.

Our knowledge of Rosewell's interior is fragmentary. The plan has been reconstructed and shows that the main entrance gave access to a great hall from which a magnificently molded and carved stair ascended. According to one member of the family who knew the house in its prime, the stair was viewed as "an object of admiration to all who saw, or ascended it, and looked down upon the large hall, with its wainscotted walls of mahogany,

and pilasters of Corinthian order, and the great hearth and marble mantelpiece." To further enrich the effect, the wainscoted walls were hung with imported tapestries.

For all Page's position and land, Rosewell proved to be a heavy drain on his income. When he died unex-

The Governor's Palace at Williamsburg was constructed c. 1706–20 and burned in 1781 while being used as a hospital during the Revolution. The present structure is a careful reconstruction based on documentary research and archaeology. (Colonial Williamsburg Foundation)

pectedly in January of 1730, the house was unfinished and his debts exceeded the value of all his slaves and personal property. Rosewell, described in his will as the "mansion house" then under construction, was left in the care of his widow, who in turn passed it to her son, Mann Page II, who probably assumed responsibility for the house and his father's debts upon reaching his majority. In 1744 he successfully petitioned the House of Burgesses to break the entail on 27,000 acres of his inheritance that

he wished to sell to satisfy these debts.

Mann Page II appears to have lived a fairly retiring life at Rosewell. In the mid-1760s, however, he erected another mansion called Mannsfield in Spotsylvania County. Of this house (destroyed during the Civil War) the architect Benjamin Henry Latrobe observed, "Mr. Page's house is built of stone of a good but coarse grit in the style of the Country Gentleman's house in England of 50 years ago. It is a tolerably good house but the taste

Rosewell in decline. By this time the original deck-on-hip roof, cupolas, and parapet had been replaced by the low hip-roof shown here. The flanking structures have also disappeared, although the small building to the right may be a fragment of the kitchens or stable. Photograph by Huestis P. Cook, 1890s. (Valentine Museum)

In this highly conjectural bird's-eye view of Rosewell in its prime, the late Thomas T. Waterman reconstructed the cupolas, parapet, deck-on-hip roof, the dependencies, walls, and garden that were removed or destroyed in the 1830s. The connecting passageways may never have been built. (Colonial Williamsburg Foundation)

Roger Hudson's house at Sunbury, Surrey, as illustrated in Colen Campbell's Vitruvius Britannicus (London, volume II, 1717). Such plates provided precedents for country houses throughout the British Empire. Copies of Campbell's book are known to have been in Virginia country house libraries. (Colonial Williamsburg Foundation)

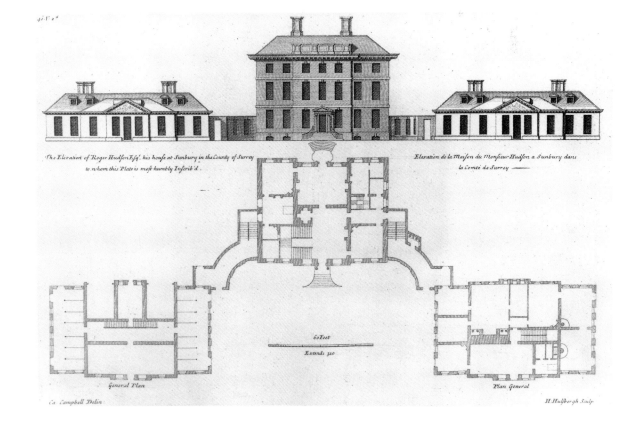

Although the original woodwork, mantels, flooring, and furnishings had long been removed, this photograph of the Rosewell great hall gives some sense of the scale of the space and the stair. (Valentine Museum)

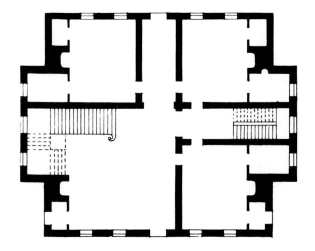

First-floor plan of Rosewell as reconstructed by Thomas T. Waterman. (The Athenaeum of Philadelphia)

is indifferent." Stone country houses of architectural pretension are unusual in colonial Virginia, and it is possible that Page was influenced by the handsome stone Mount Airy (c.1748–58). His wife was Anne Corbin Tayloe, sister of John Tayloe II who built Mount Airy.

With Mannsfield completed, Mann Page II turned Rosewell over to his son, John Page (1744–1808), who had not been sent to England to be educated because his father felt that several Virginians had recently returned from there "so inconceivably illiterate, and also corrupted and vicious, that he swore no son of his should ever go there, in quest of an education." Even without a European education, John developed strong interests in science and became president of the Society for the Advancement of Useful Knowledge in Williamsburg. He successfully calculated a solar eclipse and experimented in recording rainfall, by his own admission ". . . the first that ever were made of this Kind in America. . . ."

Young John Page found Rosewell to be in poor repair and planned in 1771 "to put it in a saving Condition next Spring." We have little way of knowing how extensive these repairs were, but like his father before him, John Page was often in debt. He had written to his agent in 1769, ". . . no Body hates the Thoughts of being in Debt more than I do: but the Great Scarcity of Money here, the shortness of my Crops for four Years past, & the

Mount Airy was erected by John Tayloe II (1721–1779), brother of Anne Corbin Tayloe Page, wife of Mann Page II, of Mannsfield. Widely considered to be one of the most significant Palladian country houses in America, Mount Airy was the home plantation for several farms totaling approximately 8,000 acres of cultivated land on both sides of the Rappahannock River. John Tayloe's son attended Eton and Christ Church, Cambridge, and became the richest man in Virginia in the early nineteenth century. Mount Airy remains in the Tayloe family. (HABS, photograph by Jack E. Boucher)

necessary Expenses of an increasing Family joined to the Commencement of Housekeeping in a large House, have forced me to submit to it for a while."

For all the trappings of aristocracy and the self-satisfaction that comes with wealth and power, many of the planters of colonial Virginia supported the break with England when it finally came. The Pages were no exception; John opposed Crown policy in the Council, then as a member of the revolutionary Committee of Safety, and subsequently as a United States congressman and governor of Virginia. His brother, Mann III, who had succeeded to Mannsfield, sat as a member of the House of Burgesses from Spotsylvania and subsequently represented Virginia in the Continental Congress.

Virginia went on to supply four of the first five presidents of the United States: George Washington of Mount Vernon, Thomas Jefferson of Monticello, James Madison of Montpelier, and James Monroe of Highland-

Ash Lawn. But more than one plantation owner might well have wondered what they had wrought by severing the legal ties to Great Britain. Seven years of the War for Independence had taken its toll in burned plantations and disrupted trade; the Anglican Church had been disestablished, and tobacco culture began to decline without free access to British imperial markets.

Mann Page III sold Mannsfield in 1808, the same year his brother John died. John's widow lived on at Rosewell until her death some thirty years later, at which point the house was sold, stripped of its lead roof, paneling, marble paving, and mantelpieces. The garden walls — including those around the Page family tombs — were demolished for the bricks, and the allée of cedars was cut for timber. Having been made to yield up most of its value, the husk of Rosewell passed through several hands in the nineteenth century until its ultimate destruction by fire.

Montpelier, country house of President James Madison (1751–1836), was erected c. 1755–65 by his father and sold by his impoverished widow in 1844. William du Pont, Sr., acquired the property in 1901 and greatly expanded the house, turning the 2,700-acre farm into a gentleman's estate. (National Trust for Historic Preservation, © Maguire/Reeder, Ltd.)

Westover on the James River was erected in 1730–34 by William Byrd II. The house burned in 1748–49 and most of the existing interiors date from after the fire. The east dependency was destroyed during the Civil War; it was rebuilt and both dependencies attached to the main block of the house by new hyphens during extensive remodeling in 1900–1905. (HABS photograph)

The Pages were not the only wealthy planter family abuilding in the 1730s. Mann Page's fellow Council member William Byrd II (1674–1744) began construction of his mansion at Westover, destined to become one of the most celebrated country houses in America. His father, William Byrd, had established the family in Virginia and by 1683 had reached the Council. In 1688 he purchased the Westover tract for £300 and 10,000 pounds of tobacco and erected a wooden farm house. William Byrd II was in London when he learned of his father's death in 1704. Returning to Virginia, he began to embellish the grounds at Westover. In 1709, he was appointed to the Council. It is probably at that time that he installed the extraordinary gates that still may be seen at Westover.

Byrd's letters and diaries from his years in England show that he had a critical eye for architecture, and he doubtless took a lively interest in the construction of the new Governor's Palace, which began shortly after his return. He records in 1711, "I walked to the house that is building for the Governor where he [Spotswood] showed me an abundance of faults and found great ex-

The Westover entrance gates were probably imported from England and installed by William Byrd II, c.1711. (Photograph by Willie Graham)

ception to the proceedings of the workmen." As the Palace was nearing completion, Byrd returned to England, where he arrived just in time for the publication of Colen Campbell's *Vitruvius Britannicus*, the subscriber's list of which included several of his English acquaintances, including the Duke of Argyle, William Blathwayt, Dr. Samuel Garth, the Earl of Islay, the Earl of Loudon, the Earl of Orrey, the Earl of Orkney, the Earl of Oxford, Sir Edward Southwell, and Sir Hans Sloane — portraits of five of these men would later hang in the library at Westover.

The rage for building Palladian country houses was gaining momentum. Byrd purchased the first two volumes of *Vitruvius Britannicus*, Leclerc's *Traité d'Architecture*, and Halfpenny's *Practical Architecture*. He eventually came to own thirty architectural books, and during his several extended visits in England spanning the years 1701–25, he made a point of viewing the latest advances in English architecture. A taste for and understanding of architecture was considered part of a gentleman's education in the eighteenth century. If every owner of architectural pattern books did not become an amateur architect like Thomas Jefferson, they at least took an active role in selecting designs and overseeing the work of their master builder or architect.

In 1726 Byrd returned to Virginia with a new wife who promptly began delivering children. ("I know of nothing but a rabbit that breeds faster," Byrd confided to his mother-in-law in 1729.) At about this time he began seriously to contemplate building an appropriate seat for his family. In 1729 he declared, "in a year or 2 I intend to set about building a very good house." The resulting two-story, Flemish-bond brick house with a steep hipped roof (four slopes instead of two) and dormer windows sits prominently on its terrace above the James River. The seven-bay horizontality of both the river and garden

The English Portland-stone doorway surrounds at Westover are justly considered among the most important—and often copied—features of the house. The design of the river-front door shown here derives from William Salmon's Palladio Londonensis (London, 1734). Recent research and physical examination suggest this door and a similar one on the garden front were added c.1750 when William Byrd III renovated the house following the fire. (Photograph by Willie Graham)

façades are interrupted by the Portland stone doorways, the most prominent features of these façades. For all their academic purity and skillful execution, however, these doorways proved to be oversized for the house.

William Byrd III succeeded to Westover in 1749 upon reaching his majority. The house he inherited, however, according to the *Virginia Gazette*, was in early 1749 "burned to the ground, with the loss of all the furniture, clothes, plate, liquore." Recent studies suggest that the fire was not as serious as the *Gazette*'s report claims, and that young Byrd extensively refurbished the house before moving in with his new wife, Mary Willing Byrd of Philadelphia. Unfortunately he had none of his father's financial acumen and gambled away most of his inheritance. By 1769 he was insolvent and on New Year's Day, 1777, committed suicide, leaving his widow to sell off such assets as his father's extensive library. Through prudent management she saved the estate for her children. The Marquis de Chastellux recorded a few years later, "She has preserved his beautiful house, situated on the James River, a large personal property, a considerable number of slaves, and some plantations which she has rendered valuable. . . . Her care and activity have in some measure repaired the effects of her husband's dissipation, and her house is still the most celebrated and the most agreeable in the neighborhood."

Westover escaped serious harm during the Revolution, but following Mrs. Byrd's death in 1814 it passed through several hands and was occupied and devastated by McClellan's army during the Civil War. In 1898 it was purchased by Mrs. Clarice Sears Ramsay, who set out to create "the most faultless example of eighteenth century architecture and furnishing in America," an effort that included rebuilding the dependency destroyed dur-

ing the Civil War, connecting both dependencies to the main house with hyphens, and replacing fireplace surrounds with copies of high-style English examples. The house was later sold to Richard Teller Crane, United States ambassador to Czechoslovakia during Woodrow Wilson's administration. For three generations Westover has been the home of his family and is now occupied by Mr. and Mrs. Frederick Fisher III and their children.

Both Rosewell and Westover were significant departures from the structures erected by prosperous planters of the previous century. Modern archaeology suggests that seventeenth-century planters lived in unframed "Virginia style" houses with walls formed by placing upright wooden posts directly in the ground without a brick foundation and with wooden ("Welsh") rather than brick chimneys. (Both Rosewell and Westover replaced earlier wooden farm houses, whose structures were probably erected late enough to have had fully framed walls on brick foundations.) The chronic labor shortage during the seventeenth century in the American colonies had worked against erecting even modest wooden-frame houses on brick foundations, let alone all brick structures. William Fitzhugh warned an English friend planning to come to America that he would

> . . . not advise to build either a great or English framed house, for labor is so intolerably dear, & workmen so idle and negligent that the building of a good house, to you there will seem unsupportable, for this I can assure you when I built my own house & agreed as cheap as I could with workmen & as diligently took care that they followed their work notwithstanding we have timber for nothing, but felling and getting in place, the frame of my house stood me in more money . . . than a frame of the same dimensions would cost in London. . . .

This changed as landowners with large holdings who used mainly slave labor began to emerge in the late seventeenth and early eighteenth centuries. (Black slaves constituted 7 percent of the population in 1690 and 20 percent by 1720.) Robert Beverly reported in *The History and Present State of Virginia* (1705), "the private buildings are of late very much improved; several Gentlemen of late having built themselves large Brick Houses." It would be interesting to know which houses Beverly had in mind — perhaps the brick houses of Jamestown or Robert "King" Carter's Corotoman, although the latter is generally assumed to have been constructed after 1705. Significantly, the emergence of "large Brick Houses" appears to coincide with the formation of the planter aristocracy, widely believed to have occurred in the early eighteenth century, especially as the demand for tobacco began to rise again after 1715, reaching its peak prosperity in the 1730–50 period.

The new country houses, such as Rosewell and Westover, reflected the increasing wealth and power derived

The depredations suffered by Westover during the Civil War are suggested in this painting by the American landscape artist Edward Lamson Henry (1841–1919). The burned dependency was reconstructed in the early twentieth century. (Corcoran Gallery of Art)

from the land. They also expressed the separation of classes that was the consequence of greater reliance on slave labor and the crystallization of what had been a fluid social system typical of frontier settlements. As the gap between masters and servants widened, there was a greater need to insulate the planter's family from the ever larger and, perhaps, threatening body of laborers and the middle managers who increasingly would be required to oversee them. Simultaneously, activities necessary to the daily sustenance of the entire plantation population were moving out of the manor house, increasing distance between owner and laborers. These evolutions had direct impact on the plan of Virginia houses of the eighteenth century.

The traditional British house plan revolved around a "great hall" as the center of all activity and to which master, servant, and guest alike had ready access directly from the outdoors. The Georgian center-hall house adopted by the "better sort" of colonial society in the early eighteenth century helped to order the social relationships between the plantation owner, his peers, and inferiors. The hall provided a reception area that became heavily laden with symbols of the owner's wealth, power, prestige, and legitimacy: richly carved woodwork, ornate stair, marble floors; family portraits and even hatchment displaying coats of arms. How far into the house the approaching visitor might penetrate would be determined by his status in the eyes of the master. A social inferior might not get beyond the hall; after conducting his business he could be ushered out, presumably impressed by what he had seen. A social equal or superior would be conducted to the more private parts of the house, while receiving the same message about his host. These entrance halls play an important role in two of the most important country houses to survive from the first half of the eighteenth century.

Like George Washington's Mount Vernon and Thomas Jefferson's Monticello, Stratford Hall has for decades prompted reverential essays and hushed voices, a carryover from the time when historic buildings were preserved for their association with great men. The eyes of a million tourists have worn these houses so smooth that they've lost their edge to delight and inform. Yet Stratford Hall is one house that casual visitors and historians alike agree upon. For architectural significance, historical association, and sheer satisfaction there are few eighteenth-century American country houses to compare with the seat of the Lee family.

Stratford Hall is today a museum in transition. It is too grandly furnished to portray accurately the Lee family residency at any period, and recent research has shown that it was erected c. 1738 rather than in the 1720s — the earlier date permitted the claim that two signers of the Declaration of Independence, as well as the Confederate leader Robert E. Lee, had been born there. All the same, Stratford is preeminent among eighteenth-century American country houses. The Lees, even those brought to Stratford as children, thought of the imposing house on the banks of the Potomac as home. There could not be a more appropriate memorial to one of America's leading colonial families.

Richard Lee (1613–1664) arrived in Virginia as a clerk and followed the now familiar path from modest beginnings to colonial aristocracy: he married well, acquired land, and prospered. He probably never thought of himself as anything but an Englishman, however. Using the profits from his American ventures, he purchased Stratford Langton, in Essex, England, which he was not able to enjoy; he died in Virginia at the age of fifty-one.

Like his father, Richard II (1647–1714) married well and added his wife's inheritance to his own. He became

a member of the Council, was appointed Naval Officer of the Potomac, and settled at a plantation called Machodoc, approximately ten miles from the future site of Stratford Hall. In quick succession the Lees produced four sons who survived to adulthood. (Among the colonial families of Virginia, the Lees were particularly blessed with good genes. Throughout the seventeenth and eighteenth centuries, each generation produced several sons who proved to have good constitutions and keen minds.)

It is Thomas Lee (1690–1750), younger son of the third generation, who interests us here. He attended William and Mary College, became Lady Catherine Fairfax's agent for the Proprietary of the Northern Neck — King Carter's road to wealth in the previous generation — and married the heiress Hannah Ludwell; they settled in at Machodoc in 1722.

On the night of January 29, 1729, however, some disgruntled indentured servants set fire to Machodoc, and the Lees barely escaped with their lives. Several years before, Thomas had purchased a 1,100-acre plantation nearby known as The Cliffs, which included a manor house built c.1670 in typical Virginia post-in-ground fashion. Whether the Lees moved to The Cliffs in 1729 or lived elsewhere remains a mystery. It has long been assumed that Stratford Hall was erected on The Cliffs

Stratford Hall (c.1738) with two of its four dependencies viewed from the south. The house was acquired in 1929 by the Robert E. Lee Memorial Association, Inc., and restored in the early 1930s with the assistance of Fiske Kimball of Philadelphia as an "enduring testimonial to the stainless life and glorious services of our departed general. . . ." (Author's photograph)

plantation to replace the burned Machodoc plantation, but a reexamination of the Lee papers and scientific dating of wood (dendrochronology, or dating by tree rings) used in the construction of Stratford Hall strongly suggest that the house dates from 1738, when it was erected by master builder William Walker under contract to Thomas Lee.

Stratford Hall is built in the form of a large *H*. Each arm of the *H* is a good-sized center-hall, four-room Georgian house, the sort that might have been found throughout the upper South in the eighteenth century. What is so extraordinary about Stratford Hall, however, is that these two houses are joined by a monumental great hall that creates a nine-bay façade over ninety feet long. The main floor is raised over a high basement, and at the point where the roofs of the two arms and the hyphen join, there rise two massive, clustered chimneys. At each

The floor plan of Stratford Hall clearly shows how the cross bar formed by the great hall connects the two arms to form the distinctive shape of Stratford, typical of the Elizabethan H-plan houses. It may also have been influenced by the plan of the Virginia capitol in Williamsburg of 1701–1705. (Robert E. Lee Memorial Association, Inc.)

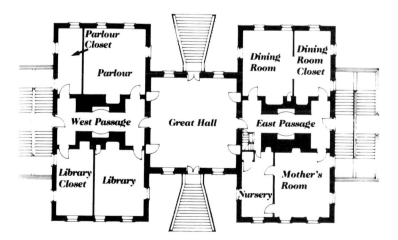

Portrait of Thomas Lee (1690–1750), builder of Stratford. (Robert E. Lee Memorial Association, Inc.)

Detail of the distinctive arched and clustered chimneys of Stratford Hall. (Author's photograph)

corner of the house is a dependency; the larger pair on the south side create a forecourt and the pair to the north, or river front, used originally as a school and office, are set at right angles and flank the view across lawns and fields to the Potomac River in the distance.

The center great-hall hyphen between the two arms is recessed by thirteen feet on both sides to form courts from which stairs rise nearly nine feet to the principal floor. Having mounted one of Stratford's main exterior stairs, the visitor enters the great hall to encounter the full force of Thomas Lee's message to the world. The great hall at Stratford was probably always intended as a reception area or, as Sir Henry Wooton recommended in his *Elements of Architecture*, "for Feasts and other Jollities." The walls are fully paneled in painted wood with Corinthian pilasters set on pedestals. Above the capitals a full entablature runs completely around the room, and

Looking past the north dependencies toward the Potomac River. (Author's photograph)

above that a ceiling shaped like an inverted tray rises to seventeen feet from the floor. It appears the room was never heated (there are no fireplaces and no trace of stove flues), and the twenty-nine-foot-square space was sparsely furnished, containing, according to Thomas Lee's inventory, a chandelier, two couches, twelve chairs, two walnut tables, and books in the glass-front closets.

The family portraits were probably excluded from this inventory; we do know they were there in 1790 when Thomas Lee Shippen visited the house and wrote to his father in Philadelphia, calling Stratford "a place of which too much cannot be said, whether you consider the venerable magnificence of its buildings, the happy disposition of its grounds, or the extent and variety of its prospects." He continues,

> What a delightful occupation did it afford me sitting on one of the sophas [*sic*] of the great Hall, to trace the family resemblance in the portraits of all my dear mother's forefathers — her father & mother grand father & grandmother and so upwards for four generations! Their pictures have been drawn by the most eminent English artists and in large gilt frames adorn one of the most spacious & beautiful Halls I have seen.

The wings of the house are bisected by passages that lead to the family reception rooms, dining room, and principal bedroom. There is no grand interior stairway at Stratford connecting the ground-floor kitchen, counting room, and secondary bedrooms to the main floor above; only a narrow, winding stair provides service access. The ground-floor bedrooms — several of which were designated by their colors in Lee's inventory (red, green, blue, white) — provided ample space for visitors and the eight children of Thomas and Hannah Lee who lived to maturity.

The massive Portland-stone steps are a re-creation of the late 1930s based on fragments discovered on the site. (Author's photograph)

When Thomas Lee died in 1750, Stratford passed to his eldest son, Philip Ludwell Lee (1726–1775), who, together with several of his brothers, was abroad, reading law at the Inner Temple in London. He appears to have been a conservative and rather austere figure — his younger siblings would later petition to have him removed as their guardian. Nonetheless, Philip Ludwell Lee would bring Stratford its greatest prosperity and elegance. He moved the plantation out of land-exhausting tobacco and into wheat, erected a public landing and mill on the Potomac, built the coach house, and established a stable. During the quarter century prior to his death and the outbreak of war, Stratford came as close to being an English country estate as anything in America.

Philip opposed the coming Revolution. Not so his five younger brothers, whom John Adams called, "that band of brothers, intrepid and unchangeable, who like the Greeks at Thermopylae, stood in the gap in defense of their country, from the first glimmering of the Revolution on the horizon, through all its rising light, to its perfect day." It was Richard Henry Lee who introduced the resolution in the Continental Congress "that these United Colonies are, and of right ought to be, free and independent States, that they are absolved from all allegiance to the British Crown, and that all political connection between them and the State of Great Britain is, and ought to be, totally dissolved." Both Richard Henry

and his brother Francis Lightfoot signed the Declaration of Independence; Thomas Ludwell Lee served on the revolutionary Committee of Safety; and the youngest sons — William and Arthur, who had been living in London, where William failed in a bid for election to the House of Commons — served the new American government in diplomatic posts on the continent.

In the meantime, Stratford passed on Philip Ludwell Lee's death in 1775 to his wife and ultimately to their daughter Matilda, who married her cousin, Henry "Light-Horse Harry" Lee (1756–1818), hero of the Continental army and future governor of Virginia. Following Matilda's death, he married Ann Hill Carter of Shirley, who became the mother of Robert Edward Lee, born January 19, 1807, at Stratford.

Unfortunately, Light-Horse Harry was a better soldier than farmer. His speculations in land backfired, the market had dropped out of tobacco (although the home plantation at Stratford had long been switched to grain crops), and he was imprisoned for debt. His son by his first wife, Matilda, was also dogged by ill fortune; his only child died in a fall (the second Lee child to be claimed by the great hall steps at Stratford); his wife consequently became a morphine addict; and after selling Stratford, they both died in poverty in Paris and are buried in unmarked graves.

Robert E. Lee would fondly recall Stratford in later years. At the depths of the Civil War, with Arlington confiscated, he wrote to his wife, "In the absence of a home, I wish I could purchase Stratford. That is the only other place I could go to, now accessible to us, that would inspire me with feelings of pleasure and local love. You and the girls could remain there in quiet. It is a poor place, but we could make enough cornbread and bacon for our support, and the girls could weave us clothes. I wonder if it is for sale, and how much."

Used mainly as a ceremonial space, the great hall at Stratford is fully paneled in painted wood with Corinthian pilasters. In the eighteenth century this room was unheated, probably had no curtaining at the windows or (as correctly shown here) carpeting on the floor. Furniture would have been arranged around the walls to be drawn out into the room as needed. (Photograph by Richard Cheek)

The parlor at Stratford reflects a Federal remodeling, probably during the reign of Henry "Light-Horse Harry" Lee, whose portrait by Gilbert Stuart hangs over the fireplace. Much of the furniture seen here and throughout the house was a gift of Caroline Clendenin Ryan in 1976. One of the few Lee objects in the house is the Federal secretary that once belonged to General Robert E. Lee. (Photograph by Richard Cheek)

Stratford was not the only country house that Robert E. Lee remembered fondly. The other was Shirley, his mother's childhood home on the James River, "a spot where I passed many happy days in early life, and one that probably I may never visit again." By the time Ann Hill Carter came as a bride to Stratford in 1793, Shirley had been in her family for five generations. Her father's maternal great-grandfather, Edward Hill I, had received a patent for it in 1660. His great-granddaughter, Elizabeth Hill, who inherited Shirley when her older brother,

Edward Hill IV, died, married John Carter (1696–1742), younger son of Robert "King" Carter of Corotoman. Thus did the powerful Carter family establish itself at Shirley.

John and Elizabeth Carter raised tobacco at Shirley and imported numerous slaves, landing them directly at their own wharf. They probably lived in a house erected on the plantation by Edward Hill I, and until recent archaeology proved otherwise, it had been thought that that house survived into the mid-nineteenth century.

The dining room is furnished with mid-eighteenth-century English objects of the type that Thomas Lee might easily have imported, although nothing shown here is known to have been in the house. The portraits are of George III (by Allan Ramsay) and Queen Caroline (by Charles Jervas), c.1730. Thomas Lee's inventory lists "one red and white marble table & frame" and fourteen chairs in this room. (Photograph by Richard Cheek)

The principal (and only) bedroom on the main floor is now known as the "Mother's Room," where family tradition holds that Robert Edward Lee was born; the crib is thought to be the one he used. The bedstead is incompletely furnished with a reproduction toile. (Photograph by Richard Cheek)

Shirley was erected c. 1738–40 by John and Elizabeth Hill Carter, and originally included a pair of flanking dependencies—all facing the James River. Shirley is located approximately halfway between Richmond and Williamsburg, Virginia. (Photograph by Willie Graham)

Only recently has it been realized that the present complex is but part of what the Carters created c.1738–40.

The modern visitor to Shirley approaches the house from the east, passing through a rigidly symmetrical service court formed by four dependencies: "granary," "ice house," "kitchen," and "laundry." The eighteenth-century visitor, however, might have approached from the opposite or river side and would have encountered the present house flanked by a pair of three-story brick dependencies sixty by twenty-four feet in plan, set back slightly to fall in line with the east façade of the central block. All three buildings may have been connected by open passages. In sheer mass the new seat of the Carters must have been more impressive than any other tidewater country house of its period, fully as grand as its exact contemporary, Stratford. It was to be rivaled only by ill-fated Middleton Place (built c.1755 and burned during the Civil War) in South Carolina, which consisted of a three-story central block flanked by a pair of two-story dependencies.

The four symmetrically placed service buildings create a forecourt to the east of the main house. (Photographs by Willie Graham)

The central block of Shirley and the four dependencies to the east are all that remains of the original composition, the northern dependency having been demolished c.1826–50 and its mate to the south in 1868. Nonetheless, Shirley is an extraordinary house for its relatively modest size. Forty-eight feet square, five bays wide on the main façades with broad windows, the two-story brick block is capped by a mansard roof—an unusual form in America at the time—pierced by large dormers with pedimented roofs. At the roof peak is a stylized "pineapple" finial, a form that evolved from the Middle Eastern pomegranate, ancient symbol of hospitality.

John Carter died in 1742, shortly after the completion of Shirley, and his widow married Bowler Cocke. They occupied Shirley off and on until their deaths a few months apart in 1771. At this point Elizabeth's son, Charles Carter (1732–1806), came into full possession of Shirley. (Already a man of considerable means, he would by the 1780s be recorded as owning property in nine Virginia counties, 785 slaves, and 815 head of cattle.) A description of the house in 1773 tells us that it was "falling into decay" and that Charles Carter intended to move there as soon as he could restore the property to proper condition.

It is now believed that in the early 1770s Charles Carter had the present woodwork installed throughout the interior and added the two-story porticoes, the most striking feature of both the east and west façades. In the 1830s Charles Carter's grandson replaced the steps and posts of the porticoes, thereby giving them the vaguely Greek Revival look they have today. (A controversy has raged for the last half century among historians who enjoy

---

Middleton Place on the Ashley River in South Carolina boasted a three-story central block that predated Henry Middleton's ownership, flanked by two large dependencies he added, c.1755. Center of a 50,000-acre network of rice plantations worked by 800 slaves, Middleton Place was burned during the Civil War. This sketch by Paolina Bentivoglio Middleton (c.1841) is one of the few documents that give an idea of its appearance. In 1857 a newspaper article described it as "adorned with the richest productions of the painters' and the sculptors' arts, with gallery of fine family portraits, by artists of high fame, and by many rare curiosities from Russia and elsewhere. . . ." (Middleton Place Foundation)

The two-story porticoes at Shirley were added by Charles Carter in the 1770s, one of the earliest uses of this distinctive Palladian motif in America (although probably predated by Drayton Hall [c. 1738–42] near Middleton Place on the Ashley River). The steps and columns were replaced in the 1830s. (Photograph by Willie Graham)

debating such matters as to whether these porches date from the original construction of 1738–40 or later. Recent research and archaeology suggest that the two-story porches are *not* original to the house but replace earlier and smaller, unroofed brick porches.)

The interior of Shirley is divided into four rooms on each floor. But unlike Westover and the later central-passage houses, Shirley has a great hall that suggests Rosewell, the Governor's Palace, and — in terms of social use if not design — Stratford. The principal feature of the fully wainscoted hall with its Gothic quatrefoil fret cornice is the grand stair. Probably based on plate 77 from William Halfpenny's *The Art of Sound Building* (London, 1725), a copy of which is known to have been in William Byrd's library at Westover, the stair rises without apparent support and has lost none of its ability to delight and amaze the viewer. Like the hall at Stratford, this room was unheated; what appears to be a fireplace is a sham, intended only for ornamental purposes.

The two rooms overlooking the river have probably always been the parlor and dining room, the fourth room having long been used as a bedroom. The parlor is easily the most elaborate space in the house: wainscoted with carved mantel and over-door woodwork boasting a curved and broken pediment with carved pineapple. The adjoining dining room is somewhat less embellished than the parlor. The baseboards, chair rail, cornice, and window surrounds are *en suite* with the parlor, but the fireplace is plain and shorter and the over-door woodwork simpler, with straight broken pediments with carved urn finials.

Shirley came through the Revolution unscathed, although nearby Berkeley was pillaged by the British under Benedict Arnold. It also escaped the worst effects of the postwar decline in the tobacco market. Charles Carter had already begun raising wheat rather than tobacco, a pattern followed by his grandson, Hill Carter (1796–1875), who succeeded to Shirley after the death of his father and grandfather. Hill Carter served during the

War of 1812 as a midshipman aboard the *Peacock* and saw action against the *Epervier* in 1813. Upon his return he married Mary Randolph and settled down to make Shirley's 1,000-acre home farm nearly self-sustaining. Corn and wheat were the principal cash crops and virtually all livestock and vegetables needed for the plantation were raised there. In an age of large families, the Carters were exceptionally prolific: they had seventeen children.

We have some idea of what the house was like in the mid-nineteenth century from no less an observer than Julia Gardiner Tyler, the fashion-conscious, outspoken

The great hall at Shirley boasts one of the most handsome stairways dating from the colonial period in Virginia. After three steps up to a small landing, it rises in two long flights, the latter of which is free hanging. (Photograph by Willie Graham)

wife of former President John Tyler who lived nearby at Sherwood Forest plantation. " 'Shirley' is indeed a fine old place, but if it were mine I should arrange it so differently," she reported in 1854 after a visit.

I should at least have the parlor in better taste and in conformity with modern fashion. Old & fine portraits all round the rooms for four generations back and *coats of arms* is over two doors of the hall as in old English style. It seemed like perfect affectation, or dislike to spend money, or bad taste that everything should remain so *old fashioned*, even to the fixtures of the tea and breakfast tables, and yet there was a crowd of every *necessary* thing — and yet it cannot be on account of the *expense* that no change is made where it can be avoided, as we know how liberal the Carters are in other respects.

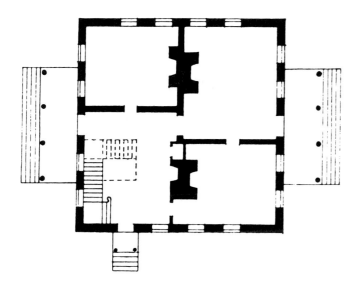

First-floor plan of Shirley. (The Athenaeum of Philadelphia)

An earlier and far less critical visitor was the impressionable Henry Barnard, who stayed there in 1833, shortly after his graduation from Yale. His description of life at Shirley seems fairly typical of pre–Civil War country house life in the South. "When you awake in the morning," he reports, "you are surprised to find that a servant has been in and without disturbing you, built up a large fire, taken out clothes and brushed them, and done the same with your boots, brought in hot water to shave, and indeed stands ready to do your bidding." Breakfast with the family followed at eight o'clock at a "table of rich mahogany, each plate standing separate on its own little cloth." Mrs. Carter presided over the coffee and tea, sending "by two little black boys as fine a cup of coffee as you ever tasted, or a cup of tea — it is fashionable here to drink a cup of tea after a cup of coffee." The host, meanwhile, "has a fine cold ham before him of the real Virginia flavor; this is all the meat you will get in the morning, but the servant will bring you hot muffins and corn batter cakes every two minutes; you will find on the table also loaf wheat, hot and cold corn bread."

Following breakfast, guests were left to their own devices: "horses are ready at their command"; or "there are books enough in the library"; or "fire and writing materials are in his room." From breakfast until "an hour or two before dinner, which is usually at three," the Carters went about their own business.

If company has been invited to dinner, they will begin to come about one — ladies in carriages and gentlemen on horseback. After making their toilet the company amuse themselves in the parlor; about half an hour before dinner the gentlemen are invited out to take grog. When dinner is ready (and by the way Mrs. Carter has nothing to do with setting the table, an old family servant, who for 50 years has superintended that matter, does it all) Mr. Carter politely takes a lady by the hand and leads the way into the dining room, and is followed by the rest, each lady led by a gentleman.

As at breakfast, both host and hostess served, Mrs. Carter at one end of the table "with a large dish of rich soup" and Mr. Carter at the other "with a saddle of fine mutton." Placed strategically for the guests to help themselves were "ham, beef, turkey, duck eggs with greens, etc. — for vegetables potatoes, beets, hominy."

Between dinner and dessert, sparkling wine was served, the first tablecloth removed, and then plum pudding, tarts, ice cream, West Indian preserves, and peaches in brandy appeared. "When you have eaten this[,] off goes the second table cloth, and then upon the bare mahogany table are set the figs, raisons and almonds, and before Mr. Carter are set two or three bottles of wine, madeira, port and a sweet wine for the ladies." The host filled his own glass first and pushed the decanters on. "After the glasses are filled, the gentlemen pledge their services to the ladies, and down goes the wine; after

Like the great hall, the parlor at Shirley is fully wainscoted and much more elaborately carved. Unfortunately, most of the eighteenth-century Hill-Carter furniture was sold at auction in the early nineteenth century. (Photograph by Willie Graham)

The connecting doorway between the parlor and dining room is surmounted by a scrolled pediment and pineapple finial. (Photograph by Willie Graham)

the first and second glass the ladies retire and the gentlemen begin to circulate the bottle pretty briskly." After rejoining the ladies for "music and a little chitchat" everyone left.

Hill Carter served in the Virginia senate and lost a bid for the United States Congress in 1843. A fervent supporter of states' rights, he joined the Confederate army along with six of his sons, one of whom died at Chancellorsville; his eldest son and the heir to Shirley, Robert Randolph Carter, was a blockade runner. Shirley itself had a number of close calls during the conflict. Nearby Berkeley plantation suffered occupation again, this time by Union forces under the command of General George McClellan. In her memoir of life at Shirley during the war, Robert Randolph Carter's wife, Louise Humphries Carter, recounted how her brother-in-law, Beverley Carter, had slipped through Union lines to reach his mother's deathbed:

> . . . if discovered, he would certainly be shot for a spy. Beverley said he must have a little sleep before riding back to Malvern Hill, and laid down on a single mattress and I sat and watched him leaning against the banisters. Just about day, I heard the tramp of steps on the walk and soldiers knocking on the shutters with their muskets and calling out, "There was a rebel spy in the house and they must have him out." Beverley went up in the cockloft, and I pulled beds and stuff before the door to hide it, then put his boots and pistols in my bed, etc., and got in there with them. Presently, eleven men came in and one taking a small silver candle stick from Papa held it in my face and said, "Excuse me, mam, I just want to see if you are a man or a woman." Then they searched the closet and other rooms and were going down stairs when Annie, who was in a perfect rage, said "O,

The dining room at Shirley has a
plain mantel, in contrast to the
drawing room, and the broken pediment over-door detailing is simpler.
(Photograph by Willie Graham)

here's a place a man might hide, better look in here."
So they pulled away the old screen and beds and
went up in the cockloft. When Bev heard them, he
crawled on his hands and knees to the other side of
the large chimneys. They were soon satisfied and
came down. . . . When they moved the guard from
this house and put them around the kitchen, I called
Beverley down to make his escape. . . . Then he went

out of the window and down the lightning rod to the
ground, dislodged the insulators and the rod fell, but
not with him. He went round the foot of the garden
to the stable, got on his horse and rode off.

The war cost Shirley its labor force and severed its
owner's access to the halls of power. But unlike the plantations of the Deep South that had been committed to

single, labor-intensive crops, such as cotton, sugar, rice, and tobacco, Shirley raised wheat and corn that could be profitably brought in with the help of small numbers of wage laborers, especially by using Cyrus McCormick's reaping machine, which had come into large-scale production by 1847. Hill Carter proved to be an excellent farmer, even without the use of slave labor, and there are testimonials to how well he avoided slipping into the debt that plagued so many of his tidewater neighbors.

Hill Carter lived on at Shirley for a decade after the war. In drafting his will, he expressed the hope "that my son Robert will leave his part of Shirley to a Carter so that it will not go out of the family of Carters at least for another generation after himself." Robert and Louise had two daughters who produced no heirs. Consequently, Robert R. Carter provided that the last surviving daughter "shall have power to vest the entire remaining estate . . . to an heir that she may select from among the descendants of my father Hill Carter bearing the name of Carter." The last surviving daughter, Marion Carter Oliver, died in 1952. Faithful to the terms of her father's will, she bequeathed Shirley to her cousin's son, Charles Hill Carter, Jr., who together with his children represent the ninth and tenth generations of the Hill-Carter family to occupy the estate that they still operate as a self-sustaining plantation.

3

V ILLAS ON THE
S CHUYLKILL

The waters of the Schuylkill River rise from the springs and snow melt of the Pocono Mountain foothills and course through loam deposited by eons of decaying oak and pine, nurturing the acid-loving rhododendrons that grow wild wherever the native forest thins. To the steep banks of this awkwardly navigable river Philadelphians have come for centuries to escape their city and, in the eighteenth and nineteenth centuries, to build country houses.

On these same riverbanks, early-nineteenth-century Philadelphians erected the first American waterworks, while other entrepreneurs developed the parklike Laurel Hill Cemetery, which soon became a public pleasure ground. By the mid-nineteenth century, industrialization threatened to encroach on the river and to pollute the water on which the city depended. Consequently, the city swept vast areas of Schuylkill watershed into the

public hands; the Centennial Exhibition of 1876 was celebrated here and, ultimately, the land became the site for the largest urban park in the world, nearly 9,000 acres stretching from the waterworks at the very heart of the modern city to the winding reaches of Wissahickon Creek. Located within the confines of this park are some of America's most important surviving colonial and early national period buildings.

On the whole these houses are best described as villas — a term used in the first century by the Roman Pliny the Younger, who described his villa near Ostia on the Tyrrhenian Sea as being "seventeen miles from Rome, so it is possible to spend the night there after necessary business is done." This is the essential characteristic of a villa: that it be erected in the country, within a day's travel from a city, yet far enough away to escape the crowds and disease of the city. By the late seventeenth

The lower reaches of the Schuylkill River as depicted by William Groombridge in 1793. In the distance is William Hamilton's The Woodlands, of which William Birch wrote, "It is charmingly situated on the winding Schuylkill, and commands one of the most superb water scenes that can be imagined." (Preston Morton Collection, Santa Barbara Museum of Art)

century, the term was in use in England, where Roger North, in his *Treatise on Building* (c.1695), defined a villa as "a lodge for the sake of a garden, to retire to enjoy and sleep, without pretence of entertainment of many persons." In eighteenth-century England it had come into common currency, according to Johnson's *Dictionary*, as a seasonal dwelling in the country, generally of smallish, symmetrical, and classical character. (It is still possible to see mid-eighteenth-century villas along the banks of the Thames at Richmond and Twickenham erected by those country families who felt compelled to maintain a presence in London or by Londoners who wanted a country house close to the city; these areas are now so built up, however, that it requires considerable imagination to evoke the once semirural character of the area.) In Philadelphia the term was in use by the late eighteenth century. Robert Morris, in writing to William Morris from his house on the banks of the Schuylkill in 1795, remarked, "I have just parted with my little visitor, he is gone to the neighboring villa. . . ."

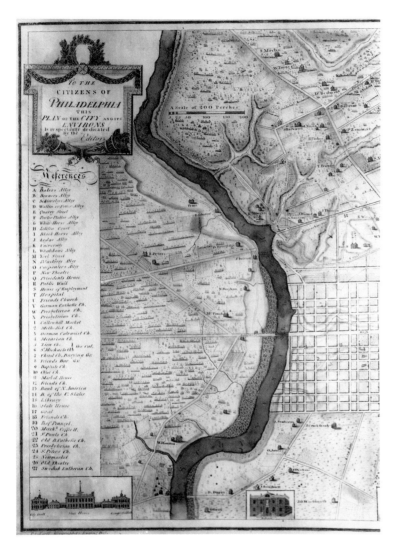

Villas along the Schuylkill near Philadelphia had already begun to appear in the 1790s when Peter C. Varlé published this map of the area. The next two decades would be the heyday of villa construction. (Historical Society of Pennsylvania)

Villas were erected for several reasons, but matters of health and comfort seem paramount. Pliny described one of his villas as being "at the very foot of the Apennines, which are considered the healthiest of mountains. . . . The summer is wonderfully temperate, for there is always some movement of the air. . . ." To eighteenth- and nineteenth-century Philadelphians, healthful air was a major concern. In 1793, to cite but one of several possible examples, the city suffered a severe outbreak of yellow fever. Dr. Benjamin Rush, Philadelphia's most prominent physician, advised those with the means to leave. Thomas Jefferson, residing nearby, reported to James Madison in Virginia that "everybody who can, is flying from the city, and the panic of the country people is likely to add famine to the disease."

Physicians were at a loss to deal with the yellow fever and cholera epidemics that regularly descended upon the city. Little wonder. Germ theory had not yet been advanced, the role of insects and rodents in spreading disease was unknown, and treatment for the victims—usually consisting of bleeding and purging—was often worse than the disease. Dr. Rush and his European-trained colleagues believed that the source of the 1793 fever was noxious air that had been infected by "some damaged coffee, which putrefied on a wharf," while others thought it had been passed by contact with refugees from Santo Domingo. In fact, that summer had been unusually wet, leaving many stagnant pools in which the female *Aëdes aegypti* mosquito could breed, sallying forth to bite infected refugees and spread the contagion. Prudence dictated that those who could afford to flee Philadelphia's nearly tropical summers should do so; in 1793 alone, 10 percent of the population of Philadelphia died.

While providing its owner with escape from the stressful and often life-threatening city on which his wealth depended, the villa also offered opportunity for

the display of wealth and property. By the early nineteenth century, few of the Schuylkill villas were out of sight of one another. Designed to provide pleasurable gardens and distant views, these houses were open to the healthful, cooling country breezes and could be seen and appreciated as features of the landscape in which they were placed. A visitor on the eve of the American Revolution records, "The country round [Philadelphia] is very pleasant and agreeable, finely interspersed with genteel country seats, fields and orchards, for several miles around, and along both the rivers for a good many miles." Artful design of house, site, and garden delighted the owner and passerby alike.

Villas were sited and designed to take full advantage of distant vistas, so that "the mind, fatigued by the agitations of the city, will be greatly restored and comforted, and be able quietly to attend the studies of letters, and contemplation," as the Italian architect Andrea Palladio had suggested in the sixteenth century. Windows were to be large, and "French" doors began to appear at ground level, to allow owners easier access to gardens, "which are the sole and chief recreation of a villa." Likewise, the orientation of a villa was supposed to take into account the prevailing winds to allow for cross ventilation. These points are fundamental to Palladio's designs for the Italian Veneto, which profoundly influenced English and, ultimately, American villa design.

Not surprisingly, given the rigors of the North American climate, particularly the heat of the Atlantic and Gulf coasts, verandas that provided shelter while allowing maximum enjoyment became increasingly important in the design of villas. "Through them comes the view of pleasant twilights, and the evening breezes blow sweetly among the climbing plants that cover them," according to one account.

As Roger North suggested in 1695, "a villa is . . . for the sake of a garden." Unlike the country houses built upon plantations, these villas presided over relatively modest tracts of land that rarely provided anything beyond some of the daily fare at their owners' tables. Setting was all, and the garden — created as transition between house and landscape — became increasingly important.

Accomplished amateur architect
Thomas Jefferson worked on Monticello near Charlottesville, Virginia,
from 1768 through 1809, although
the main features of the house date
from the period after he returned
from duty in Paris as United States
minister in 1789. (HABS, photograph by Walter Smalling)

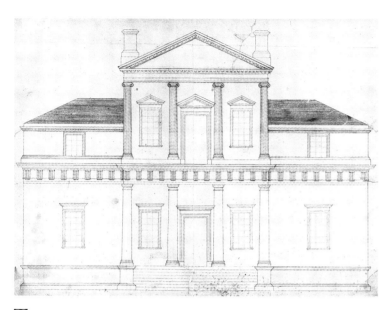

Thomas Jefferson used a Palladian two-story portico on the final design (1771) for the first version of Monticello. Architectural historians cannot agree whether the second level of the portico was actually built. The octagonal projections Jefferson added to the wings are not shown on this drawing, only on the plan. (Massachusetts Historical Society)

Jefferson's Monticello on its mountaintop above Charlottesville, Virginia, is often called a villa because it was so influenced by Roman villa design. But isolated as Monticello was, it is not correct to label it a villa. Nonetheless, listen to Jefferson attempting to coax Maria Cosway to visit him at Monticello: "where has nature spread so rich a mantle under the eye? mountains, forests, rocks, rivers. With what majesty do we there ride above the storms! How sublime to look down into the workhouse of nature, to see her clouds, hail, snow, rain, thunder, all fabricated at our feet! and the glorious sun, when rising as if out of a distant water, just gilding the tops of the mountains, and giving life to all nature!"

The largest and most elegant pre-Revolutionary house in the Philadelphia area was Lansdowne, country villa of John Penn. In 1753, Penn had come to Pennsylvania from England, and a few years later married Ann, daughter of Chief Justice William Allen. Penn began assembling in 1773 a tract of land on the west bank of the Schuylkill near Philadelphia that would eventually reach two hundred acres. The house he began to build that year is gone and little known today, but had Lansdowne survived, it would be ranked among the most significant Palladian houses of the late colonial era in America. Unfortunately, only two representations of the house executed before its destruction in 1854 are known to exist. There is a watercolor by the English artist James Peller Malcom supposedly dating from 1792, and the far more detailed view from William Birch's *Country Seats of the United States of North America* (Philadelphia, 1808). Birch is a reliable delineator; he shows

Design for a two-story, pedimented portico from Andrea Palladio's The Four Books of Architecture, *as illustrated in the London 1738 edition.* (The Athenaeum of Philadelphia)

Lansdowne, erected by Pennsylvania Governor John Penn, Sr., on the eve of the American Revolution, "lies upon the bank of the Pastoral Schuylkill, a stream of peculiar beauty, deservedly the delight and boast of the shores it fertilizes," according to William Birch, who published this view in his Country Seats of . . . America (Philadelphia, 1808). (The Athenaeum of Philadelphia)

John Adams referred to Mount Pleasant as "the most elegant country seat in the Northern colonies." Erected on 160 acres overlooking the Schuylkill in 1763 by the Scot privateer John Macpherson from designs by master builder/architect Thomas Nevell, the house remains largely unchanged, except for the surrounding landscaping, which is more typical of early-twentieth-century colonial revival gardens than of actual eighteenth-century gardens. (HABS, photograph by Jack E. Boucher)

a two-and-one-half-story, stuccoed stone house with quoins, water table, belt course, and denticulated cornice. There is nothing unusual here, nor in the low roof pierced by internal chimneys with a flat deck surmounted by a balustrade, which can be found at nearby Mount Pleasant (1763) and Woodford (second story c.1772) or the John Vassal (Longfellow) House in Cambridge, Massachusetts (1759).

Two features of Lansdowne, however, stand out immediately: the two-storied pedimented portico that dominates the Schuylkill River (east) façade and the projecting bays of the north and south façades. The influence of Palladio is apparent in the pedimented porticoes. In both his *Four Books of Architecture* and in his own executed designs — such as Villa Pisani, which greatly influenced Thomas Jefferson's early sketches for Mon-

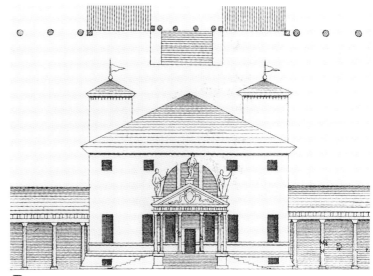

Palladio's use of clustered columns is illustrated in this plate from The Four Books of Architecture. *(The Athenaeum of Philadelphia)*

Woodford (c.1756) acquired its second floor and most of its celebrated Palladian architectural features c.1772. *(Author's photograph)*

ticello — Palladio popularized a two-storied pedimented portico with Ionic columns on the lower level and Doric columns above. The "colossal portico," where columns rise without interruption from porch floor to roof, is popularly associated with the colonial house, but virtually all of those known in America are actually post-Revolution additions to earlier structures, such as William Hamilton's spectacular Woodlands (which was remodeled in 1787–90) or the better-known Mount Vernon (which was expanded in 1777–84).

Lansdowne's portico is not the earliest of the two-story type in America; similar examples had already appeared at Drayton Hall (1738–42) and the Miles Brewton House (1765–69) in South Carolina. In place of the usual American practice of four-over-four columns supporting the pediment, however, Penn's architect adopted the less common and doubtless more expensive style of

paired columns on the corners of the portico, rising from a truncated pyramid of steps. The projecting bays on the flank elevations are an even more unusual feature for the time. Similar projecting bays appear at Monticello in the 1771 design and at William Buckland's superb Matthias Hammond House (1774–75) in Annapolis, Maryland.

The architect or master builder of Lansdowne is unknown, as is true for most late colonial houses in America. The sophistication of the design points strongly to one of the masters of The Carpenters' Company, such as Robert Smith (1722–1777), Benjamin Loxley (1720–1801), or Thomas Nevell (1721–1797), yet no buildings by these three, all of whom were middle-aged by the 1770s, is similar to Lansdowne. A more likely candidate is a man from the next generation, particularly William Williams (1749?–1794), who advertised in the *Pennsylvania Packet* a few months before Penn began to build in 1773:

William Williams, a native of this city . . . begs leave to inform his friends, and the public, that having lately returned from London, where he has for some time studied architecture in its various branches, he proposes carrying on the business of House Carpentry in the most useful and ornamental manner, as is now executed in the city of London, and most parts of

England; and humbly hopes, from his practice and experience, to give the highest satisfaction to such as shall be pleased to employ him, in a new, bold, light and elegant taste, which has been lately introduced by the great architect of the Adelphi Buildings at Ducham Yard [Robert Adam]; and which is now universally practiced all over Britain.

Williams's advertisement is one of the earliest Philadelphia references to Adamesque neoclassicism. Williams is known to have owned English architectural books that were new in the 1770s, such as N. Wallis's *A Book of Ornaments in the Palmyrene Taste Containing Upwards of Sixty New Designs* (London, 1771), which survives in the library of The Carpenters' Company. He served in the American army during the Revolution, rising from captain to lieutenant-colonel; following the war he resumed his trade. Williams is known to have worked on such neoclassical structures as Library Hall, the President's house, and Congress Hall. He died in 1794, probably from yellow fever.

John Penn of Lansdowne was governor of Pennsylvania on the eve of the American Revolution, but he did not flee when the Continental Congress and the Committee of Safety took control of the government. Except for a brief period of imprisonment prior to the fall of Philadelphia to the British army in 1777, he seems not to have been disturbed. For all the depredations suffered by Tory and Rebel alike from the shifting fortunes of war, the American Revolution was no class struggle, and few loyalists were executed during or after the hostilities. For most of the war, John Penn lived quietly at Lansdowne and his city mansion, biding his time until the conflict at arms was resolved one way or the other.

To John Penn, Jr. (1760–1834), grandson of Pennsylvania's founder and younger cousin of John Penn of

Lansdowne, the defeat of the British army and the resulting recognition of the new United States promised to be cataclysmic. He had never been to America, but his family had depended for a century on the income derived from their proprietary rents and sales of land in Pennsylvania—interests the new government had sequestered. In the hope of recovering his inheritance, he journeyed to Philadelphia in the summer of 1783, a few months after the signing of the preliminary treaty of peace between Britain and the United States of America. It is probable that Penn intended to make a permanent home there if the family claims—estimated to be worth the staggering sum of £944,817—proved successful, but for the moment he lived with his older cousin in an elegant town house—later to become the Philadelphia residence of President George Washington—and at Lansdowne overlooking the Schuylkill.

America impressed John Penn, Jr., at first. He later wrote, "I felt, indeed, the accustomed '*amor patriae*,' & admiration of England, but sometimes a republican enthusiasm . . . attached me to America, & almost tempted me to stay." Finding it unpleasant to live under his older cousin's roof, Penn purchased fifteen acres on the west bank of the Schuylkill for £600. The house he designed and built on this land was only a short ride from his cousin's villa Lansdowne; it should be seen as the private retreat of a wealthy young bachelor—what he called his "villa near Philadelphia"—rather than the country seat of a man who laid claim to three-quarters of the Penn inheritance.

Penn named his new house after the Duke of Württemberg's La Solitude, "a name vastly more characteristic of my place," he wryly remarked. Erected in 1763–67 by Duke Karl Eugen von Württemberg as a hunting lodge, La Solitude is in the forested environs of Stuttgart. Penn visited the *Schloss* while on a grand tour following

Schuylkill River façade of The Solitude today. (Author's photograph)

The Solitude by engraver William Birch from his Country Seats of . . . America. "Here a pleasing solitude at once speaks the propriety of its title . . . , the solitary rocks, and the waters of the Schuylkill add sublimity to quietness." (The Athenaeum of Philadelphia)

his graduation from Cambridge and just before his trip to America, recording:

> . . . arrived at Stuttgard. I made a three days stay to see the town, & two country-palaces, called La Solitude, & Ludwigsburg. La Solitude owes its present beauty to the reigning Duke. The approach is noble. It is about a mile thro a park & two gates in it, the sides of the road being woody & overgrown, & between the trees are discerned deer of various kinds, feeding, & tame wild boars. The buildings are detached. There is one long parlour by itself in one part. Out of sight stands the main body, containing only

about 8 rooms, fitted up in the richest manner, but tempered, as it were, by elegance.

Something about La Solitude struck a chord with young Penn; perhaps it was isolation or the small number of rooms "fitted up in the richest manner but tempered . . . by elegance." Yet The Solitude bears little physical resemblance to its German namesake, which is many times larger than Penn's villa.

Penn read widely in landscape and aesthetic theory — he owned a copy of Edmund Burke's *On the Sublime and Beautiful* (1756), for example. Commenting in his letters on the proportion to be observed between house and view, Penn noted the attraction of "irregular gardens" as well as "regular ones," with vistas through "*voûte d'arbus*" which he called "picturesque." While he lacked at The Solitude a view "over an immense tract toward the city & surrounding fields" as could be found at European palaces, the elevation of his site "occasions an effect much beyond little contrivances."

We know more about Penn's villa and its grounds than is typical for more than a few eighteenth-century properties in America. The layout of Penn's fifteen acres has come down to us in the form of the surveyor John Nancarrow's "Plan of the Seat of John Penn." The house and its detached kitchen — connected by an underground passage — occupy a knoll overlooking a stream flowing into the Schuylkill below the house. To the east and south the trees have been cut to provide appropriate vistas from

the principal rooms. A winding path begins at the east front of the house, cutting down the hill to the riverbank, parallel to the "ha-ha" ditch designed to confine grazing animals, across the stream and through the woods to the flower garden. From this point guests might retrace their steps or, perhaps if ladies were not present, continue on to the road that brought the stroller to the kitchen garden and "The Wilderness" with its informal paths leading to the bowling green or, through the *allée* of trees that screened the bowling green from the approach road, back to the house.

Guests arriving at The Solitude by carriage or horse-

West façade of The Solitude today. Restored and furnished for the Bicentennial, the house was open to the public for a decade. It is now used as offices by the Philadelphia Zoo. (Author's photograph)

Portrait of John Penn, Jr., by *Robert Edge Pine (1730?–1788).* *(Private collection)*

back would dismount to be greeted by their host in an oval courtyard. The house itself is a modest cube twenty-nine feet wide by twenty-nine feet deep with two-and-one-half floors that Penn carefully worked out to be twelve, ten, and seven feet high, although he appears not to have allowed for joists and rafters between floors, so the overall height exceeds twenty-nine feet. This symmetrical exercise, undiminished by projecting wings or sheds, seems perfectly scaled to site and to the human pleasures and purposes its owner had in mind. It is the ideal villa for a single occupant of taste and solitary disposition who expects his guests to go home in the evening.

Buff-colored stucco scored to simulate rectangular

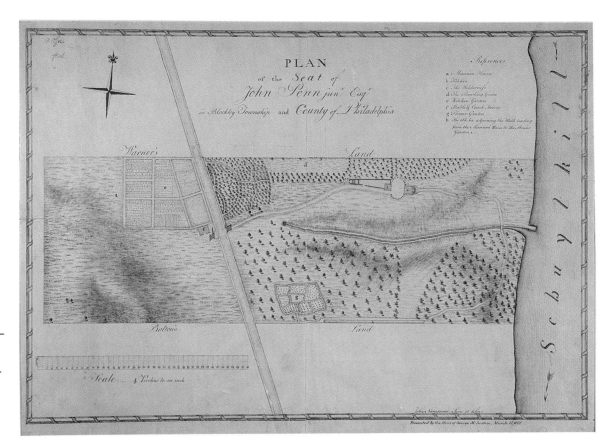

Plan of the Seat of John Penn *junr. Esqr. . . . ," by John Nancarrow, c. 1784. (Historical Society of Pennsylvania)*

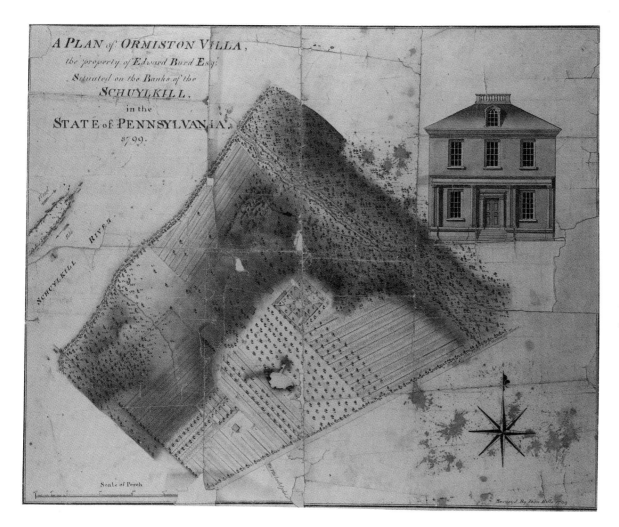

A Plan of Ormiston Villa, the property of Edward Burd Esqr: Situated on the Banks of the Schuylkill, in the State of Pennsylvania, 1799." by John Hills. Believed to have been constructed in 1798, this villa is typical of modest Philadelphia-area houses influenced by The Solitude. (Historical Society of Pennsylvania)

blocks of cut stone covered the exterior walls, setting off the white wood trim. There were no exterior shutters. The main or west entrance frontispiece, with its triangular pediment and attached columns with Ionic capitals, is typical Philadelphia work of the time. The east façade, however, features a single-story portico surmounted by decorative urns, which echoed the roof balustrade with its urns. This feature was unusual in Philadelphia and was soon adopted in various forms in the porticoes of such structures as Edward Burd's Ormiston Villa dating from 1798.

It seems likely that Penn served as his own architect; certainly the preliminary plans done in his hand that lay out the interior space seem to be the work of an amateur;

the layout was only slightly improved in execution by his carpenters. Separation of the kitchen from the house by a forty-foot underground passage offered the practical advantage of protection from fire as well as odors and noise, though it also ensured that most food would not arrive at the table hot. Similarly, the division of space on the second floor with its bewildering warren of doors provided an isolation from the comings and goings of household servants more normally associated with much larger establishments. Penn's demand for privacy must have bordered on obsessive.

Each floor of The Solitude is designed around a single room. On the ground floor this is the parlor, which Penn tells us is "entered into thro a jib-door." (A jib door is constructed to be flush with the wall, without moldings and decorated in the same way as the walls of the room so as not to be obvious.) There is consequently no grand entrance to the parlor; rather, it is necessary to enter a "small lobby" that is "divided from the hall by a green-baize [covered] door." Across the east wall of the parlor, opposite the fireplace, are two French "glass-doors conducting into the Portico" and the view of the Schuylkill beyond.

Erected by George Thompson in 1810 and acquired by the city of Philadelphia in 1869, Rockland is one of the most elegant surviving villas of the Federal period in America. Its neglect by indifferent city officials borders on the criminal. (Author's photograph)

Ground-floor of The Solitude near Philadelphia - 12 high.

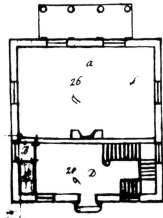

a . Parlour, entered into thro a jib-door, glass-doors conducting into the Portico —
B . Small lobby, divided from the hall by a green-baize door —
C . Closet entered from the lobby thro a wooden do —
D . Hall —

Second Floor of the Solitude near Philadelphia - 10 high.

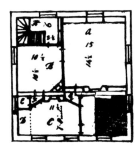

a . Library, entered thro a glass door, matching the other doors for books and pictures
B . Bed room.
C . Do
D . Alcove for a bed.
E . Closet.
F. G. Small lobbies or passages between the doors.
H. Closet, & Roof-story stairs.

Roof-story of the Solitude near Philadelphia - 7 high.

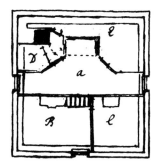

a . Best room of this story, with an Alcove-bed —
B . Space or thoroughfare to ascend upon the leads & to which bells communicate.
C . Room lighted by a glass-door, & to contain a servant's bed.
D. E. Two dark closets.

John Penn, Jr., drew these plans for his villa, The Solitude, in his "Commonplace Book" (c.1784). "Earlier in the year," he records, "had made a dear purchase of 15 acres, costing £600 sterling. . . . I gradually altered my scheme to the great increase of the expenses it put me to." (Historical Society of Pennsylvania)

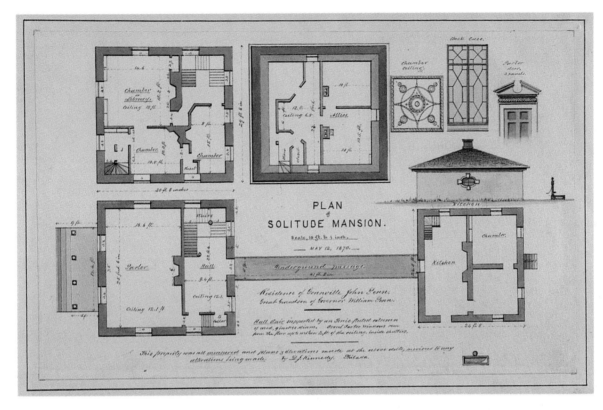

PLAN
of
SOLITUDE MANSION.

The second floor is designed around the library, "entered thro a baize & glass door, matching the other doors for books round the room," where Penn kept his library of several hundred volumes, including works on architecture by Robert Morris (*Select Architecture*, 1757), Batty Langley (*The Builder's Complete Assistant*, 1766), and Abraham Swan's *The British Architect*, which had been reprinted in Philadelphia in 1775. With an elegant plaster ceiling, the library has floor-to-ceiling bookcases with glass doors that were built in and fortunately survive today. The floor originally was covered with a large ingrain or "Scotch" carpet, and presumably this is where Penn kept his "writing table standing on brass castors, with 3 drawers on each side."

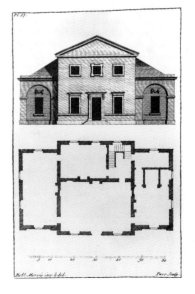

Inspiration for The Solitude most probably came from the center of this plate for "a little Building intended for Retirement or for a Study, to be placed in some agreeable Part of a Park or Garden" from Robert Morris's Select Architecture. Penn's inventory of his American library included a copy of the 1757 edition. (The Athenaeum of Philadelphia)

Typical of late-eighteenth-century practice, the parlor at The Solitude could be used as a dining room. In addition to the twenty-six mahogany chairs covered in striped horsehair, Penn's inventory—on which this refurnishing is based—included a "large semicircular side board table, in which are three drawers, the middle drawer divided into eleven partitions, leaded for liquors; 1 large dining table and 2 semicircular tables to fix at each end, which 2 being put together form a round table of themselves." (Philadelphia Museum of Art)

The east wall of The Solitude parlor, with its French doors leading out to the portico, as refurnished during the Bicentennial by the Philadelphia Museum of Art. The inventory of Penn's furniture from the house lists three "elegant large settees having [horse] hair bottoms, with satin stripe, a double row of gilt nails and fluted legs," all in the "modern fashion." There were two armchairs and twenty-four matching side chairs similarly upholstered, four "cotton and worsted [wool] striped parlour curtains, with cord," and "an elegant Wilton carpet, 20 by 12." (Philadelphia Museum of Art)

Off the library were two bedrooms: the larger bedroom was only ten and a half feet square, and that, we presume, is where Penn kept his "field bedstead on castors with sacking bottom and furniture stripe cotton curtains." Next door an even smaller bedroom contained a sleeping alcove furnished with plate-printed cotton curtains depicting William Penn's treaty with the Indians.

Penn later complained of suffering "the vanity of English taste, in furnishing & decorating the house" so el-egantly, especially after he learned that Pennsylvania had no intention of restoring the family's rights to their former rents and lands. He bitterly complained that they had been "robbed" and "almost branded as thieves." Consequently, he ordered the contents of his new house sold at public auction in the spring of 1788, and he sailed for England. He never returned to his villa on the Schuylkill. Penn, who was said to suffer from a "nervous affection" that "was sometimes distressing to himself and others,"

The marble mantels of The Solitude are believed to have been imported from England. Penn also owned "1 pair elegant dining room brass andirons, with polished steel shovel, tongs and hearth brush," and a "large oval looking glass in a gilt frame" that may have been similar to those shown here in the refurnishing of the house by curators of the Philadelphia Museum of Art. (Philadelphia Museum of Art)

The alcove bed and windows were dressed with a "set of hair colour furniture cotton bed curtains, pattern William Penn's treaty with the Indians; 3 window curtains to match ditto, with cord, tassels and screws." (Philadelphia Museum of Art)

The entrance hall at The Solitude is long and narrow, its most dramatic feature being the wrought-iron balustrade of the stair, which probably was fabricated in Philadelphia. The circular ends of the dining table may have been kept here, together with many of the chairs, which could be brought in when the parlor was set for dining. (Philadelphia Museum of Art)

*F*ollowing *Penn's return to England,* Poems by John Penn, Esq *(London, 1801) appeared, in which he included this view of The Solitude, "the villa near Philadelphia . . . built by me, while I resided in America," after a painting by Robert Edge Pine. (Library Company of Philadelphia)*

died a bachelor in 1834. The Solitude passed to his younger brother, Grandville Penn, and from him to Grandville John Penn, who visited the house briefly during his triumphal visit to America in 1851, when he gave a *"fête champétre"* on the grounds for his local hosts. During the 1860s when Fairmount Park was being assembled, The Solitude was acquired by the city; it is now surrounded by the Philadelphia Zoo.

Rejection of the Penn petition by the Pennsylvania

*C*lose-up *of plate-printed English cotton fabric showing "William Penn's Treaty with the Indians" (c.1785), the pattern used by John Penn, Jr., at The Solitude. (Henry F. DuPont Winterthur Museum)*

The earliest known photograph of The Solitude by Robert Newell, c.1875, is taken from the southeast, the same angle adopted by Birch. The kitchen building was demolished to make way for the Philadelphia Zoo about this time. (Library Company of Philadelphia)

I never viewed myself as a tenant on any other conditions than an entire subservience to your interest and convenience. The moderate terms on which the lease was granted could imply no other species of arrangement. I therefore cheerfully resign the same, with my best wishes for your long enjoyment of Lansdowne.

But Penn appears not to have reoccupied the house, although he did return to Philadelphia. He died in 1795, leaving the property to his wife, from whom it passed to

Photographer Robert Newell also provided the only known view of The Solitude from the southwest, which clearly shows the relationship between the kitchen and the main house, c.1875. The approach road passed between the trees and the kitchen into the oval courtyard. (Library Company of Philadelphia)

Assembly led the elder John Penn to return to England as well. In 1789 he sold his household goods and leased Lansdowne to William Bingham. Bingham (1752–1804) was the richest man in America, and Abigail Adams called his wife, the beautiful and accomplished Anne Willing Bingham, "the finest woman I ever saw."

Bingham wrote of Lansdowne that "the buildings are excellent, the land good, and the local situation of the place, very agreeable and commanding." Yet, when he learned that John Penn expected to return to Philadelphia in 1792, he wrote:

it is natural to believe that you would be desirous of repossessing yourself of a country seat to which Mrs. Penn and yourself must be particularly attached. . . .

the merchant James Greenleaf. The same year Penn died, Vice-President John Adams wrote to Abigail, "went to Lansdowne on Sunday, about a half mile on this side of Judge Peter's, where you once dined. The place is very retired, but very beautiful—a splendid house, gravel walks, shrubberies, and clumps of trees in the English style—on the banks of the Schuylkill."

James Greenleaf continued to rent to the Binghams until Greenleaf went bankrupt in the economic panic of 1796–97. Bingham purchased Lansdowne, later admitting that he had "foolishly given too large a sum . . . that

he might gratify Mrs. Bingham," who was particularly fond of the house. To provide an appropriate entrance to his new property, Bingham commissioned iron gates with flanking lodges from the young London architect Henry Ashley Keeble.

In 1874 the sometime architect and watercolorist David J. Kennedy (1817–1898) recorded the site of Lansdowne, determining that the house stood 114 feet above the Schuylkill. His reconstruction of the house itself is based on the Birch engraving. (Historical Society of Pennsylvania)

Portrait of William Bingham by Gilbert Stuart (1795). (Private collection)

Portrait of Anne Willing Bingham by Gilbert Stuart (1795). Of her elegance a contemporary wrote, "she blaz'd upon a large party . . . in a dress which eclips'd any that has yet been seen. A Robe a la Turke of black Velvet, Rich White Sattin Petticoat, body and sleeves, the whole trim'd with Ermine. A large Bouquet of natural flowers supported by a knot of Diamonds. . . . Her Head ornamented with Diamond Sprigs interspers'd with artificial flowers, above all, wav'd a towering plume of snow white feathers. Can you imagine a dress more strikingly beautiful?" (Private collection)

Around the time the Binghams acquired the property, Robert Gilmor, Jr., twenty-two-year-old son of Bingham's business partner, made an extended visit. "It is a most superb place," he wrote, "and supposed to be the best country house in America. It commands a noble view of the Schuylkill and the seats in the neighborhood, and at a distance the steeples of some of the churches in Philadelphia." Yellow fever was raging in the city at the time of Gilmor's visit, and Bingham wisely kept his household in the country. Gilmor's account of his visit to Lansdowne gives a sense of Philadelphia society at the apogee of the Federal city.

A great deal of company came out to dinner today, among which were the three princes [Duc d'Orleans, Montpensier, and Beaujolais, who had just returned from a visit to the western United States]. We spent a charming afternoon and at night Mr. Bingham would not permit me to leave his house but insisted on my staying there all the time I meant to spend near Philadelphia.

I remained there about a week, passing my time in the most agreeable manner. Company were continually visiting Lansdowne, and added to its own made a most sociable society. During the day I either amused myself with hunting or retired to the library where [Gilbert] Stuart was engaged in painting the whole family. In the evening we played at the French game of the lottery, in which we were occasionally joined by the princes and viscount [de Noailles] who

staid after night. Our party was increased by the arrival of Mr. Alexander Baring (son of Sir Francis Baring) whom Mr. Bingham invited to stay in the family. He is an extraordinary young man, of great mercantile talents and possessed of much information. Though a young man of about 25, he is respected by all the old characters who know him. . . .

One day the family of the British minister, Mr. Liston, dined at Lansdowne; in his suite were Mr. Thornton, Mr. Brown, and Lord Henry Stuart, all secretaries and assistants. . . . The day passed as usual; very agreeable and the company did not sit long at table, particularly the young people who assembled in the portico and on the lawn.

While considerably larger than a typical American villa and clearly able to sustain year-round residency as

The gates and entrance lodges of Lansdowne, erected in 1798 by William Bingham from designs by the London architect Henry Ashley Keeble. This watercolor by David J. Kennedy is based on Keeble's original drawing, since lost. The lodges were actually one hundred feet apart, but Kennedy moved them closer together for the purposes of his composition. (Historical Society of Pennsylvania)

a country seat, Lansdowne was not the Binghams' principal residence. In 1786 they had erected a grand city house on South Third Street in Philadelphia. Shortly thereafter, the New England architect Charles Bulfinch reported in a letter to his parents that it "is in a stile which would be esteemed splendid even in the most luxurious part of Europe."

Elegance of construction, white marble staircase, valuable paintings, the richest furniture and the utmost magnificence of decoration makes it a palace in my opinion far too rich for any man in this country. We are told that his mode of living is fully equal to this appearance of his house. Of this we shall be better able to judge in a few hours as we are to dine there today.

"Far too rich" Bulfinch might describe it, yet he carefully copied the main façade and introduced it to Boston with his Harrison Gray Otis House (1795–96).

Urbane and literary Samuel Breck, founder and long-time president of The Athenaeum of Philadelphia, knew

*S*weetbrier, Samuel Breck's
Schuylkill River villa near Lansdowne. (Author's photograph)

the Binghams well and in 1797 erected a villa called
Sweetbrier not far from Lansdowne. Breck, who had
lived and been educated in France and was accustomed
to European fashions, said that William Bingham "lived
in the most showy style of any American"; and his diary
opens for us a small window on the Binghams' life-style.

The forms at his house were not suited to our man-
ners. I was often at his parties, at which each guest
was announced; first, at the entrance-door his name
was called aloud, and taken up by a servant on the
stairs, who passed it on to the man in waiting at the
drawing-room door.

In this drawing-room the furniture was superb
Gobelin, and the folding doors were covered with
mirrors, which reflected the figures of the company,
so as to deceive an untravelled countryman, who,
having been paraded up the marble stairway amid
the echoes of his name — oftentimes made very ridic-
ulous by the queer manner in which the servants
pronounced it — would enter the brilliant apartment
and salute the looking glasses instead of the master
and mistress of the house and their guests.

According to Breck, this "silly fashion" of announcing
names caused so many problems that it was eventually

halted. Not, however, before then-Senator James Monroe—hearing a liveried footman call his name—replied, "Coming." Then, hearing his name announced at the next level, he cried out in frustration, "Coming as soon as I can get my greatcoat off!"

Anne Willing Bingham died in 1801 when she joined a sleighing party, caught cold, and went into a rapid decline. Her husband's grief following her death caused him to leave America for England with his daughter and her husband, Alexander Baring, head of Baring Brothers and Company, the leading banking house in England. Finding himself in France at the time that the sale of the Louisiana Territory to the United States was being set in motion, Bingham joined with the Barings to finance the transaction. He suffered a stroke and died in Bath, England, in 1804. The contents of the Binghams' town house were sold at a celebrated public auction, but the Baring heirs maintained Lansdowne for their own use while in America, renting it from time to time when appropriate tenants became available. One of these provided a final moment of glory for Lansdowne.

With the defeat of Napoleon, yet another wave of French émigrés arrived in America; now marshals of France changed places with their countrymen who had come to America after the Revolution. The most celebrated of these arrived in 1815, Joseph Bonaparte, elder brother of Napoleon and former king of Spain. Landing at New York, the comte de Survilliers, as he styled himself, took passage to Philadelphia, where he rented Lansdowne while searching for an appropriate property to purchase. Eventually he chose Point Breeze on the east bank of the Delaware River near Bordentown, New Jersey. Over the next few years he assembled an estate of 1,800 acres that would be celebrated for its miles of carriage drives and gardens, magnificent collection of art and furniture, and lavish scale of entertainment.

That Joseph Bonaparte chose to settle on the Delaware River rather than the Schuylkill was probably determined by the availability of larger tracts of arable land. The river widens as it approaches Philadelphia and becomes tidal, and its banks are flat and fertile—in all a topography to encourage landed estates. It was here, twenty-five miles north of the proposed city, that William Penn's deputy governor had set aside 8,431 acres for the proprietor's use and on which Penn constructed in 1683 a brick and frame house facing the river. (The present house, operated as a museum, is a complete reconstruction by the colonial revival architect R. Brognard Okie, erected by the WPA, the original house having long been destroyed.) Over the next century and a half, the banks of the Delaware became lined with landed estates and

Lansdowne was destroyed on July 4, 1854, when boys playing with fireworks accidentally set it afire. The following year Ballou's Pictorial magazine published this view of "the ruins of a once princely mansion, the abode of wealth and luxury." The site was later cleared to make way for the Centennial Exposition of 1876. (Library Company of Philadelphia)

summer villas, many featuring handsome examples of virtually every architectural style. Unfortunately, time and industrialization have dealt a cruel blow to this rich legacy; most are gone and, with the exception of Pennsbury and Joseph Bonaparte's Point Breeze estate near Bordentown, most have been forgotten. There is, however, a notable exception: Andalusia.

One of the Philadelphia merchants attracted to the banks of the Delaware was John Craig, who in 1795 purchased a farm located halfway between Pennsbury and the city. Here he erected a relatively modest house in 1797–98. As Craig's fortunes flourished, he ap-

proached the fashionable architect Benjamin Henry Latrobe to improve and expand the house—which became the mansion Andalusia—although Craig did not live to see the architect's design realized. Craig died in 1807, leaving a wealthy widow with several children, one of whom, Jane, married Nicholas Biddle.

Nicholas Biddle (1786–1844) came from a respected family of means whose roots extended deeply into the earliest Quaker settlements of the Delaware Valley. Serious and bookish, he entered the University of Pennsylvania at an early age and then transferred to the College of New Jersey (Princeton), from which he was

View of Andalusia by Thomas Ustick Walter (c. 1834) before he began to enclose the house designed for the Craigs by Benjamin Henry Latrobe. (HABS, photograph by Jack E. Boucher) ▶

The Delaware River from the terrace of Point Breeze, Joseph Bonaparte's estate north of Philadelphia, by Thomas Birch. (Private collection)

what was to be a lifelong interest and appreciation of classical architecture.

After returning to practice law in Philadelphia, Biddle was elected to the Pennsylvania legislature, where he distinguished himself as an advocate of internal improvements, a regulated currency, and a national bank. He also became editor of the literary periodical *Port Folio*, wherein he published an article by George Tucker advocating the patriotic suitability of Greek architecture for America.

In 1811, Biddle married Jane Craig. Mrs. Biddle's mother died in 1814, and from the close of the War of 1812 until 1819 — when Biddle's involvement with the second Bank of the United States kept him in Philadel-

*P*ortrait *of Nicholas Biddle by Thomas Sully. (HABS, photograph by Jack E. Boucher)*

*N*icholas *Biddle met the American painter John Vanderlyn (1775–1852) while both were in Paris. He was so impressed by Vanderlyn's* Ariadne *that he commissioned a smaller version of the upper torso, which is still at Andalusia. (Pennsylvania Academy of the Fine Arts)*

graduated at fifteen. After briefly reading law, he was invited by General John Armstrong, newly appointed United States minister to France, to accompany him as secretary. During the three years he spent in Europe, Biddle witnessed Napoleon's coronation as emperor of France, met the artists Jean-Antoine Houdon and John Vanderlyn, and visited Greece, which aroused in him

The Bank of the United States, designed by William Strickland; "a chaste imitation of Grecian architecture in its simplest and least expensive form." The commission was awarded in 1818 and the building occupied in 1824. (Author's photograph)

phia — the young family moved to Andalusia in the spring and remained there almost continuously through the fall. This seems to have been fairly typical of country villa families of the eighteenth and early nineteenth centuries. Andalusia did not become a year-round residence of the family until the 1930s.

Nicholas Biddle, already a prominent figure among the elite of the largest and most urbane city in America, became president of the Bank of the United States in 1822. Around him Philadelphia basked in the twilight of Federal splendor. Among his friends he numbered artists, architects, and men of letters in addition to merchants,

bankers, and politicians. With Peter S. DuPonceau, William Tilghman, Joseph Hopkinson, Samuel Breck, and Mathew Carey, he founded the Athenaeum library in 1814 and, in 1818, the Wistar Association, a social club made up of local literary figures. According to Biddle's biographer, "this informal bringing-together of the leading Philadelphia citizens gave the city a unity and cohesiveness that seemed to be missing in other American cities and was at least partly responsible for the high quality of its public, philanthropic, and educational institutions."

Through his work with the *Port Folio*, Biddle met the

Portrait of Thomas Ustick Walter (1804–1887) by John Neagle, done in 1835. (The Athenaeum of Philadelphia)

any) direct role Biddle had in selecting the design is questionable. Certainly Biddle would have applauded the choice, and the new building is known to have given him pleasure.

Of more importance to the future of Andalusia was Biddle's association with a Strickland pupil, Thomas Ustick Walter. In the manner of most early-nineteenth-century native American architects, Walter first learned a craft; like his father, he was a master bricklayer. Trained in Strickland's office and taught drawing and watercolor techniques by the English-born architect John Haviland and the landscape artist William Mason—what Walter called a "liberal but not collegiate" education—he began to practice architecture in 1831, first gaining local attention with his Gothic-style Moyamensing Prison (1831–35) and then national recognition for the design of Girard College for Orphans (1833–48) in Philadelphia. Hundreds of commissions followed in the 1830s and 1840s, including some in locales as far-flung as Venezuela and China. It was in 1850, however, when Walter entered the competition for the design of the extension of the United States Capitol, that his place in American architecture was firmly established. The wings and dome of the Capitol would shape the image and iconography of American governmental building for a century to come and secure for Walter a place among the most important American architects.

It was the commission for Girard College that first brought Nicholas Biddle together with his future architect. Stephen Girard's bequest provided both the means and the opportunity to erect one of the grandest buildings in America, and Biddle, an advocate for Greek architecture, sat as chairman of the board of trustees. With a design based on Jacques-Anges Gabriel's eighteenth-century buildings in the Place de la Concorde, Paris,

young architect and engineer William Strickland, who won the competition for a building to house the Bank of the United States, which was to be "a chaste imitation of Grecian architecture in its simplest and least expensive form." Biddle was not a member of the board of directors when Strickland's design was submitted, and what (if

Thomas Ustick Walter's original design for Girard College. Biddle called it "large and showy," lacking in "simplicity and purity, but not ill adapted to please others." (The Athenaeum of Philadelphia)

Final design for Girard College by Thomas Ustick Walter. (The Athenaeum of Philadelphia)

Walter won the competition against entries from most of the leading American architects. Biddle thought the design "large and showy," lacking in "simplicity and purity, but not ill adapted to please others." He urged Walter to redesign the building, and the architect returned eighteen days later with a Greek peristyle temple design.

Impressed with Walter's obvious skill (and perhaps impressed by his tractability), Biddle invited him to Andalusia to expand Latrobe's house of 1806–1807. Orig-

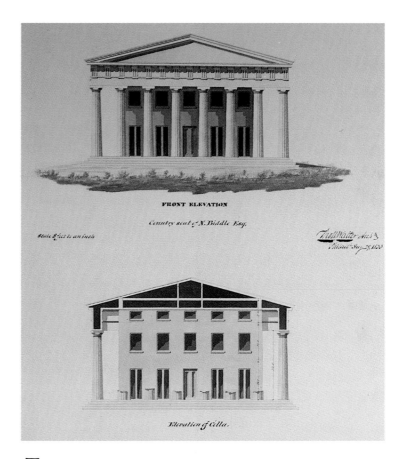

The front elevation of Walter's original design for Andalusia. (The Athenaeum of Philadelphia)

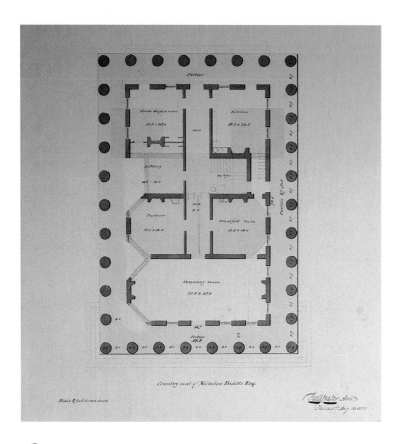

"Country seat of Nicholas Biddle" by Thomas Ustick Walter, 1833. In this plan Walter proposed to surround the house with columns. (The Athenaeum of Philadelphia)

inally, Biddle and Walter considered making the house over into a miniature Parthenon, with what architectural historians call a peripheral octastyle plan; that is, a single row of columns around the perimeter with eight across the pedimented ends. Walter, however, favored the simpler and less expensive hexastyle structure (six columns across) based on the surviving fifth-century (B.C.) Doric-style Temple of Theseum in Athens. Only Biddle had actually seen these temples, of course, but Walter owned the seminal book of American neoclassicism, James Stuart and Nicholas Revett's *Antiquities of Athens* (London, 1762, and later editions).

Work on the house progressed through 1834. On March 20, 1835, with all the columns in place, Walter rowed out to the middle of the Delaware to obtain the full effect of what he had wrought, for the main front is intended to be seen from the river. "The building shows nobly from a distance," he recorded, "the proportions of the Doric order are so massy that they require to be seen from a distance." Walter's design enveloped the Latrobe house and created two new parlors in the front, overlooking the river. Floor-to-ceiling windows permitted

easy access directly onto the porches, which the family always referred to as the piazzas. In addition, the third floor was enlarged and two-story wings added across the land-side front to provide a kitchen (to the north) and library (to the south).

The main rooms created by Walter's extension of Andalusia were the formal parlors — the "yellow" and the "ottoman" — overlooking the Delaware. Their handsome plaster ceiling medallions, cornices, and pilasters; classically detailed marble mantels; and French chandeliers have caused these rooms to be among the most published in America. In warm weather the lower sash of the windows in these rooms can be thrown up to permit direct

Temple of Theseum from James Stuart and Nicholas Revett, Antiquities of Athens *(London, 1762, and later editions). Walter owned this book, of which his teacher William Strickland had said, "the student of architecture need go no further." (The Athenaeum of Philadelphia)*

access onto the piazzas. Behind the yellow and ottoman parlors are the original parlor and dining room of Latrobe's house, which retain their original exterior windows that now open into Walter's new parlors; these contribute to the sense of openness in the suite of four rooms, none of which is unusually spacious. The interconnection of these spaces permits large groups to be entertained; yet each is so warmly intimate that a small group is equally comfortable.

In the south wing, Walter and Biddle created a new library, which contains what may be the most important surviving built-in bookcases from the neoclassical period in America. To this day they retain their original paint and gilded highlights; and on the shelves is Nicholas Biddle's extensive library, much as he left it—in all, a unique American survival.

But Walter's contribution to Andalusia did not end with the creation of the main house, which the Biddles

The west front of Andalusia. (HABS, *photograph by Jack E. Boucher*) ▶

The east, or river, front of Andalusia, showing Walter's addition. (Author's photograph)

The "yellow" parlor at Andalusia contains objects acquired by several generations of Biddles. The marble mantel is probably Italian; the white-and-gilt over-mantel mirror was made for the house in the 1830s. The chandelier was acquired from the Paris firm of Thomire & Cie by Edward Biddle as agent for his parents. The June 4, 1836, bill describes it as "Une Lampe dorée mal a douze Lumieres portier par 12 Enfans Bacchus poser sur des Modillons attacher au candeau Culor rechement orné de consoler Pavillon a consoler & pralmetter." The maple sofa table on the right, with painted slate top, carries the label of Anthony G. Quervelle, master Philadelphia cabinetmaker of the 1820s and 1830s. (Photograph by John Chew)

Adjoining the "yellow" parlor is the "ottoman" parlor, with its modern reproduction of the now destroyed nineteenth-century ottoman that gave the room its name. The bookcase desk is American, c.1790–1800, and the French ormolu chandelier was purchased by Nicholas Biddle from J. & J. Cox, New York City, on June 14, 1836. (Photograph by John Chew) ▶

promptly began to embellish with appropriate "Grecian"-style neoclassical furnishings. For the grounds, Walter was commissioned to expand the billiard house and design a suitably picturesque Gothic ruin on the riverbank, practical graperies for the garden behind the house, and a cottage for long-term guests that in the mid-nineteenth century acquired the Gothicized architectural details that have been so richly embellished in recent years by the

The red parlor contains a suite of maple furniture, probably purchased by Nicholas Biddle from a Philadelphia cabinetmaker, c. 1820–30. The curtains are twentieth-century copies of originals in the Andalusia collection. The porcelain dessert set displayed to the left of the fireplace is said to have been a gift to Mrs. Nicholas Biddle from the Marquis de Lafayette. (Photograph by John Chew)

present occupant, James Biddle, great-grandson of Nicholas Biddle.

In 1839 Biddle resigned from the Bank of the United States, expecting to spend the balance of his life raising Guernsey cattle and thoroughbred horses, cultivating grapes and the Morus Multicaulis mulberry for feeding silkworms. Black clouds of economic depression hung over the country, however, and two years later the bank

Originally the library of the Craig house, the study contains one of a pair of sling-seated armchairs purchased in 1836 for $44.00. Such "Spanish," or "campeachy," chairs were popular library furniture in the early nineteenth century; a pair had been given to Thomas Jefferson in 1819, and one survives at Andrew Jackson's Hermitage. The small portfolio cabinet to the left of the window contains a set of John James Audubon's The Viviparous Quadrupeds of North America (1843). (Photograph by John Chew)

With its wine velvet upholstery and polished mahogany furniture, the library is an inviting room. This chandelier was also purchased by Edward Biddle in 1836 for his parents. Thomire & Cie describes it as "Une grande Lampe dorée mai 18 Lumieres portier pardes branches, Culor orné de Six Enfans ailer ronde basse Pavillon richement decoré." (Photograph by John Chew) ▶

The dining room, part of the house designed by Latrobe for Mrs. Biddle's parents, retains an original window that now opens into the ottoman parlor. The marble-top mahogany sideboard may be by the Irish-born cabinetmaker Joseph B. Barry (1757?–1839), who settled in Philadelphia after the Revolution. (Photograph by John Chew)

The painted-and-gilt bookcases of the new library added by Thomas Ustick Walter are among the most important examples in the Grecian style to survive in the United States. They house Nicholas Biddle's considerable library, including his editing of the Lewis and Clark journals (1814). The sofa is wood-grained and gilt-decorated similarly to the bookcases. The statue is of Napoleon I in his coronation robes. Young Nicholas Biddle was in Paris on December 2, 1804, when Napoleon was crowned emperor, and he would later become a friend of the exiled Joseph Bonaparte, who lived at Point Breeze across the Delaware. (Photograph by John Chew)

The nearby Gothic-style Cottage was probably designed by Thomas Ustick Walter. Used traditionally as a dower house, the Cottage has been Mr. James Biddle's private residence since Andalusia was opened to the public. As shown here in the front hallway, the architectural theme has been carried to the interior wallpapers and furnishings. (Photograph by John Chew) ▶

failed — and Biddle was blamed. Even his beloved Philadelphia had lost its preeminence as America's first city to New York; the Erie Canal and the conquest of Biddle's own Bank of the United States at the hands of Andrew Jackson spelled the end.

Speaking of Biddle after his fall, fellow Athenaeum

The front parlor of the Cottage is arranged for informal entertaining and contains both inherited objects and more recent additions from several cultures. (Photograph by John Chew)

founder Sidney George Fisher would record in his diary, "there have been few instances of a more complete reverse of fortune. I was never among those who praised him or admired him extravagantly in his prosperity, and I think now that the censure, the abuse, the hatred which accompanied his downfall were quite excessive and un-

The back parlor of the Cottage serves as a library and continues the Gothic theme used throughout the house. (Photograph by John Chew)

merited as the fulsome adulation which was offered to him by the whole community during the period of his power."

Broken financially, Biddle relinquished his city house and moved year-round to Andalusia, which was saved from the maelstrom of his declining fortune by Mrs. Bid-

An enclosed porch runs across the front of the Cottage, overlooking the Delaware River. (Photograph by John Chew)

dle's trustees, who purchased Andalusia with funds from John Craig's estate. Shortly thereafter, John Quincy Adams dined at Andalusia and recorded, "Biddle broods with smiling face and stifled groans over the wreck of splendid blasted expectations and ruined hopes. A fair mind, a brilliant genius, a generous temper, an honest heart, waylaid and led astray by prosperity, suffering the penalty of scarcely voluntary error." There would be precious little time for such brooding, however; Biddle suffered from a heart condition, and on February 27, 1844, he died suddenly. Remarked Sidney George Fisher upon hearing the news, "his manner was gracious, smiling, easy, gentlemanlike, a little condescending & exhibited surpreme self-satisfaction & elation. His conversation was ready, fluent, elegant & witty. His language was always choice & happy, and without being raised above the conversational tone, without approaching the vile habit of haranguing, flowed in free sparkling & harmonious periods."

Mrs. Biddle continued to summer at Andalusia, as did succeeding generations of the family. This use protected the property from serious change, even in the furnishings. One mid-nineteenth-century description called it "a beautiful place of 100 acres on the river and much expense was lavished on it by [Nicholas Biddle] in the time of his prosperity. The house is of Grecian architecture . . . a style unfit for a dwelling, especially in the country, and therefore in bad taste, but nevertheless in itself beautiful. It is large, with many rooms handsomely furnished in the manner of thirty years ago." For sixty years following Mrs. Nicholas Biddle's death her children retained joint, undivided ownership; this helped to preserve the house from being modernized in one of the several styles of the Victorian period that obliterated so many eighteenth- and nineteenth-century American country houses. Joint ownership ended in the early twentieth century, by which time the preservation and careful embellishment of Andalusia as it had been known by Mr. and Mrs. Nicholas Biddle became a trust to be passed to future generations.

4

ROMANCE

ALONG THE HUDSON

On August 18, 1807, the sylvan quiet of the Hudson Valley between New York City and Albany disappeared forever, shattered by the pounding, belching, thrusting ascent of Robert Fulton's steamboat on its maiden voyage. One farmer who happened to observe the nighttime passage rushed home to bar the door and shutter the windows, announcing that the devil was on his way to Albany in a sawmill. The transportation revolution had come to the Hudson; an upstream trip traditionally requiring a week to ten days by sailing sloop could now be accomplished in just over twenty-four hours. And when the Hudson was linked to the Erie Canal—which by the early 1820s would snake across 363 miles to Buffalo on the Great Lakes—the primacy of New York City as gateway to the heartland of America was assured.

On its upriver journey, Fulton's *Clermont* (as it would popularly be known) made a stop at the dock of an estate called Clermont, which was owned by Robert R. Livingston. Livingston had first met Fulton in Paris and had supported his early experimentation with steamboats on the Seine. Impressed by the results, he financed the purchase of a British engine from Boulton & Watt and the construction of the New York boat. Flushed with the success of the maiden voyage, Livingston publicly announced Fulton's engagement to his cousin, Harriet Livingston, and then stepped ashore on land that had been in the absolute possession of his family since 1686.

The founder of the family in America, Robert Livingston's great-grandfather (who bore the same name as his great-grandson), had been born in Scotland in 1654 and shortly thereafter was taken to Holland by his father, a Presbyterian minister unhappy with the religious policies of the restored Stuart monarchy. By 1674 young Robert had migrated to America, where his aptitude for

John Ferguson Weir, View of the Highlands from West Point *(1862). According to Mrs. Frances Trollope, who visited the Hudson highlands in the late 1820s, "The beauty of this scenery can only be conceived when it is seen. . . . Sometimes a lofty peak shoots suddenly up into the heavens, shewing in bold relief against the sky; and then a deep ravine sinks in solemn shadow, and draws the imagination into its leafy recesses. For several miles the river appears to form a succession of lakes; you are often enclosed on all sides by rocks rising directly from the very edge of the stream, and then you turn a point, the river widens, and again woods, lawns, and villages are reflected on its bosom." (New-York Historical Society)*

business and facility with languages served him well. (The British had captured the province of New Netherland and renamed it New York a decade before, but wealthy Dutch families still dominated the colony.) Five

years later he married the widowed Alida Schuyler Van Rensselaer; the marriage provided him with connections to many of the great Hudson Valley families and access to extensive Van Rensselaer properties. For services to the government he secured a royal patent in 1686 for the Lordship or Manor of Livingston, "with full power and authority at all times for ever hereafter in the said Lordship," which included the right to convene a court and pass sentence on those who lived within his manor. He now presided with virtually absolute power over some 160,000 acres of New York wilderness, to which tenants were gradually attracted; they paid an annual rent, usually a percentage of their crops, and owed a few days' work on the lord's lands each year. Representing his own borough, Robert Livingston sat as a member of the New York Assembly and would spend most of his life defending his rights to the vast estates that were to make

erected as villas or as long-term summer residences to which the women and the younger children of the household moved in the spring even if the head of the family found it necessary to spend more of the season in the New York house, hotel, or club. One of the most interesting of these is Montgomery Place, handsomely sited on a bluff overlooking South Tivoli Bay near Annandale-on-Hudson, and erected as Château de Montgomery between 1804 and 1805 by Janet Livingston Montgomery (1743–1828), sister of Chancellor Robert Livingston of Clermont.

In the early 1760s Janet Livingston met the British army captain Richard Montgomery (1738–1775), whose boat had run aground off Clermont. Nothing came of this first meeting, but when Captain Montgomery resigned his commission and emigrated to New York City in 1772 — writing, "I have cast my eye on America, where my pride and poverty will be much more at their ease" —

his descendants wealthy — and enable them to sponsor such enterprises as Fulton's steamboat.

For all his aristocratic (some would say feudal) rights, privileges, and wealth, grandson Robert R. Livingston, Jr. (1746–1813), threw in his lot with the patriot cause during the Revolution and became a member of the committee to draft the Declaration of Independence, although he contributed nothing to the document. For his treason, Clermont was burned in 1777 by British forces. Following the war and the Constitutional Convention, Livingston — who had become chancellor of New York, the state's highest legal office — failed in his effort to be appointed Chief Justice of the Supreme Court. Instead, he became United States minister to France.

The rebuilt Clermont is but one of more than a dozen mansions erected by the Livingston family along a twenty-mile stretch of the Hudson, several of which remain in family hands to this day. Accessible by river to New York City, most of these country houses were

East front of Clermont today. (Author's photograph)

he wasted little time in reestablishing a relationship with the socially prominent and independently wealthy Janet Livingston. They were married the following year and planned to settle into genteel farming near Rhinebeck, New York. With the coming of the Revolution, however, Montgomery joined the American forces as a brigadier general. He suffered a hero's death while leading his men in the abortive New Year's Eve effort to capture Quebec in 1775.

The widowed and childless Janet Livingston Montgomery never remarried and lived on with her family at the rebuilt Clermont. But at the age of fifty-nine, she

Montgomery Place, formerly called Château de Montgomery, erected by Janet Livingston Montgomery in 1804–1805 and extensively remodeled and enlarged by Alexander Jackson Davis from the early 1840s through the late 1860s. The 1844 contract calls for "The outside of the building to be sanded, so as to look exactly like Stone." The present color scheme—shown here on the west façade—replicates that used by Davis in the later repainting: various stone colors with joints struck off with thin white lines. The shutters were dark green and the trim white. (Historic Hudson Valley, photograph by Sue Morrow Flanagan)

Alexander Jackson Davis (1803–1892), Louise Livingston's architect, would transform Montgomery Place into a neoclassical villa in the "Palmyran" style. Portrait by George Freeman (1789–1868). (Avery Architectural Library, Columbia University)

and painted white. The house and grounds were tended by twelve slaves — four adult men, two adult women, two young women, and four girls under the age of fourteen. (Slave ownership was legal in New York until 1827.) An avid gardener, Janet operated a commercial nursery on the estate and lived contentedly at the house until her death in 1828. One poignant anecdote has come down to us from these years. In 1818 her husband's remains were recovered from Quebec and returned to New York City for burial. The steamboat *Richmond*, which carried his ashes, halted on its way down the Hudson opposite Janet's house, where she stood waiting on the broad terrace. The strains of the "Dead March" could be heard from the band on board, a salute was fired, and the boat passed on — leaving behind the supine figure of the fainted widow.

When Janet Montgomery's younger brother, Edward Livingston, and his wife, Louise, inherited the house, they changed the name to Montgomery Place. As secretary of state and minister to France, Edward Livingston found little opportunity to visit his Hudson River property. He retired to Montgomery Place in 1835, planning to improve the house and grounds, but died unexpectedly the following year.

His widow, Louise (1781–1860), had been born in Santo Domingo to a wealthy planter family. Married at the age of fourteen and widowed two years later, she fled the bloody revolution of 1800 and settled in New Orleans, where she met and married Edward Livingston in 1805. Upon her husband's death, Montgomery Place once again fell into the hands of a widow with building proclivities; it was about to enter its period of greatest architectural glory.

In selecting an architect, Louise Livingston and her daughter, Coralie Livingston Barton, chose well. Alexander Jackson Davis (1803–1892), like his contempo-

purchased the 242-acre Van Benthuysen farm downriver from Clermont. She broke ground for a new house in 1804, completing the simple Federal rubble-stone-walled structure the following year. The walls were stuccoed

rary Thomas Ustick Walter, would leave an indelible stamp on American architecture in general and the emerging profession of architect in particular. A native of New York City, Davis studied art and determined early in his career to become an architect — or "architectural composer," as he styled himself at first, reflecting his primary interest in the design rather than the structural aspects of architecture. In this he differed from most native American architects who, like Walter and other successful contemporaries such as John Notman and Samuel Sloan, emerged from a craft tradition.

A superb delineator and renderer, Davis became a junior partner of the prominent architect, engineer, and intellectual Ithiel Town (1784–1844). As observed in the previous chapter, these were the years when neoclassicism reigned in America, and Davis's work in the 1830s contributed a fair number of monumental structures in this style, particularly the Indiana State Capitol (1831–35) and the New York Custom House (1833–42), both modeled on the Parthenon.

In calling Davis to Montgomery Place, Louise Livingston wrote him in 1842, "we cannot proceed without the aid of your taste, experience & skillful pencil." At the time he came to work for her, Davis had already experimented with the Gothic villa at Lyndhurst downriver, nearer to New York City, which will be visited in a moment. At Montgomery Place, however, probably at the request of his client, Davis transformed the simple Federal-style house into a classical villa in what he designated his "Palmyran" style — after the Roman ruins at Palmyra in Syria that so influenced the neoclassical movement. Typical of versatile architects of the time, Davis could work equally well in a variety of styles, and as he demonstrated at both Montgomery Place and Lyndhurst, his later work always respected the architectural vocabulary of the original design. Between 1843 and 1867

he added to Montgomery Place the now-famous octagonal pavilion to the north, a wing to the south, a porch to the west overlooking the terrace and the Hudson River below. On the east front the once modest house acquired a Corinthian portico with balustrade and urns, while the roofline was changed to accommodate a classical cornice and balustrade with a central tablet embellished with classical swags that echo the portico cornice. The entire exterior was restuccoed, painted, sprayed with sand while still wet, and given painted lines so as to look like stone from a distance.

The grounds of Montgomery Place included formal gardens, an arboretum, and a glass conservatory; miles of walks and roads; rustic seats, waterfalls, and a lake.

After Coralie Livingston Barton inherited Montgomery Place in 1860, she asked Davis to return and add the semicircular front portico and a new, more massive roof balustrade. From this proposed elevation of the east façade by Davis, it is clear that an additional floor was considered at the same time; instead, a large dormer was added to the attic on the west front. (Historic Hudson Valley, photograph by Jim Frank)

The landscape architect, horticulturist, and architectural critic Andrew Jackson Downing, who was a friend of Mrs. Livingston and her daughter, called it "one of our oldest improved seats . . . nowhere surpassed in America in location, natural beauty or landscape gardening charms."

On the eve of the American Civil War, Edward and Louise Livingston's only child, Coralie (1806–1873), inherited Montgomery Place. She had married Thomas

Pennant Barton, son of Philadelphia physician Benjamin Smith Barton, and they continued the fruitful association with Davis by commissioning the semicircular wood portico inspired by the Temple of Vesta and a new, more massive balustrade to balance its bulk for the west façade, and several outbuildings to further embellish the grounds: a coach house, farm cottage, and the romantic Swiss Cottage.

Coralie Barton died childless in 1873, and Montgomery Place, after several decades of joint ownership, passed to Maturin Livingston Delafield, who left it to his son, Brigadier General John Ross Delafield, in 1921. In 1964 the house became the residence of his son, Major John White Delafield (1905–1985), and his daughter-in-law, Anita Delafield. Anita wrote of the house in the 1960s: "Strong family tradition and the precept of saving and *never* throwing away have guided successive generations at Montgomery Place. The interests and aspirations of all its occupants live on under the towering locusts: here are still the books they treasured; the letters they wrote and read; the furnishings they collected; the china, silver, and crystal they dined from. Attic trunks yield up the

original window hangings, and even great black plush tricorn and servants' red plush and gold-buttoned bottle-green livery. In the lofty-ceilinged spacious rooms, drowsing now in the violet dusk of winter, the painted faces of these early owners still watch over their house."

The charm of Montgomery Place — and Andalusia as well — is this continuity of family care and, occasionally,

*V*iew *of the Hudson River from the terrace of Montgomery Place in winter. (Author's photograph)*

ANDERSON SC.

neglect. Here, too, is an accumulation of objects both precious and common, the sense of casual insouciance that no curator could re-create and might easily destroy. These fragile conditions make special the few surviving houses built and embellished by Americans of taste, education, and wealth who also had the sense to engage the services of creative professionals. Montgomery Place is now maintained to reflect the continuity of Livingston family ownership by Historic Hudson Valley, which took possession in 1986.

The historical parallels between the Biddles' Andalusia and the Livingstons' Montgomery Place are obvious: continuity of ownership by politically and culturally prominent families with strong ties to France,

FORRES SC.

The entry hall, with its broad arch and tapered wood colonettes, remains largely as it was in the original house of 1805, although the plaster ceiling medallion and the cast cornice were added in 1854 and the wallpaper is a twentieth-century replacement. The plaques (hanging above the doors leading to the double parlors) are after Danish neoclassical sculptor Bertel Thorvaldsen (1770–1844). (Author's photograph)

In the entry hall are several objects commemorating Edward Livingston's association with Andrew Jackson, including a portrait of the President by Ralph E. W. Earl. Here also are introduced the French Empire and American Grecian neoclassical furnishings acquired for Mrs. Montgomery by Chancellor Livingston in 1804 and supplemented by later generations. The ormolu-finished chandelier is probably the "bronze and gilt chandelier" purchased in France in 1871 for the dining room. (Author's photograph)

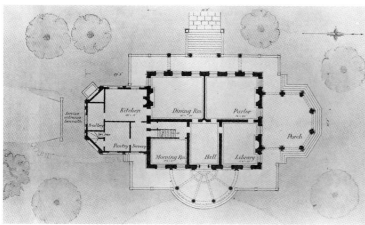

Plan of first floor, Montgomery Place, from Great Georgian Houses in America *(New York, 1933). (The Athenaeum of Philadelphia)*

The north parlor, later referred to by the family as the "yellow drawing room" because of the curtain and upholstery fabric installed there, has always been wallpapered. The floral striped paper with flocked border shown here probably dates from a mid-nineteenth-century redecoration and constitutes a rare survival. Architecturally the room remains largely unchanged from the earliest period except for the gray marble mantel installed between 1825 and 1835. The window treatments shown date from the twentieth century and replace classical draping in bright yellow moreen trimmed with blue silk bobbin fringe over gold-leaf wood poles. (Historic Hudson Valley)

The south parlor was being used as a formal dining room by the mid-nine-teenth century and is identical in size to the adjoining parlor. The portraits hanging above Janet Montgomery's New York Federal sideboard are of Mrs. Robert Livingston, Mrs. Montgomery's mother, by Gilbert Stuart, and Coralie Livingston Barton by Jacques Amans (1801–1888). The dining room chairs are believed to have been among the objects sent to Mrs. Montgomery by her brother from Paris while the house was under construction. (Historic Hudson Valley)

which are reflected in the interior decoration of the houses. In fact, when John Armstrong arrived in Paris with young Nicholas Biddle in tow to assume the post of United States minister to France, he replaced Robert R. Livingston, Jr., who was, incidentally, his brother-in-law. (One of the most ironic similarities, however, is the role of Andrew Jackson in Nicholas Biddle's decline and Edward Livingston's advancement as public figures. Both are largely attributable to Jackson's enmity or pa-

tronage.) Architecturally, both houses began as relatively simple Federal structures—villas of the eighteenth-century type that John Penn of The Solitude would have recognized. And both came to be enlarged and embellished by leading practitioners of the newly emerging American architectural profession. But even as these two houses were being converted into mature neoclassical architectural compositions, in keeping with the villa tradition as it would have been known on the banks of the Thames or the Schuylkill, a new definition of what a country villa should be was gaining currency on both sides of the Atlantic.

Two of the key figures in this change—Alexander Jackson Davis and Andrew Jackson Downing, together with most of their American colleagues—were influenced by the Scottish landscape-gardener and architectural critic John Claudius Loudon (1783–1843), who edited three journals—*The Gardener's Magazine* (1826–42), *The Magazine of Natural History* (1829–36), and *The Architectural Magazine* (1834–38)—and wrote several books that were widely read by American architects. Of Loudon's books, *Encyclopedia of Cottage, Farm and Villa Architecture* (London, 1833) was the most influential. In it he described a villa as "a country residence, with land attached, a portion of which, surrounding the house, is laid out as a pleasure ground; or, in other words, with a view to recreation and enjoyment, more than profit." Villas differed from cottages and farms, which "are occupied as the means of obtaining and enjoying the comforts of life," by the addition of "the gratifications resulting from the display of wealth and taste." Consequently, "it is not necessary that the dwelling of the villa should be large, or the land surrounding it extensive; the only essential requisites are, that the possessor should be a man of some wealth, and either possess taste himself, or have sense enough to call to his assistance the taste and judgement

of others. . . ." So far, these characteristics differ little from those of the classical definition discussed in the last chapter.

But Loudon's villa did not need to be constructed near a city, nor was it necessarily a seasonal residence. More important, he rejected the classical—"Grecian"—style traditionally associated with the villa because architecturally a villa "ought to exercise some influence on the imagination; and, therefore, whichever style may be selected, it ought always to be accompanied, as far as practicable, by such circumstances as may serve to heighten its effect on the mind." Neoclassical architecture is found wanting, he maintained, when submitted to these tests of influencing the imagination or heightening the

Villa in the Norman Style" designed by W. Russell West, Cincinnati, Ohio, from Andrew Jackson Downing, The Architecture of Country Houses *(1850). "It is highly picturesque," Downing writes, requiring "wild scenery and hills, whose pointed tops are in harmony with the strength of the heavenward-pointing round tower." (The Athenaeum of Philadelphia)*

Costing by Downing's estimate $4,600 to erect in brick, this villa in the Italian style "expresses not wholly the spirit of country life nor of town life, but something between both, and which is a mingling of both." Italianate would become the American suburban style of choice in the 1860s. (The Athenaeum of Philadelphia)

---

effect on the mind, for it has "but few associations connected with its external appearance to recommend it for the country."

While it might be argued that neoclassical architecture evokes response through association with ancient learning or political and social virtues, most critics of the nineteenth century would have maintained these were *intellectual*, not *emotional*, responses. According to Loudon, Greek or Roman architecture was "frequently adopted, merely as evidence . . . of scholarship and taste." What style, then, was appropriate for this new type of villa in the country? From Loudon, and through him from his American disciples Davis and Downing,

came the resounding answer. In Downing's words, the picturesque styles, particularly the medieval Gothic, were suited to the dynamic American people, "men of imagination — men whose aspirations never leave them at rest — men whose ambitions and energy will give them no peace within the mere bounds of rationality" — that is, within classical buildings.

These are the men for picturesque villas — country houses with high roofs, steep gables, unsymmetrical and capricious forms. It is for such that the architect may safely introduce the tower and the campanile — any and every feature that indicates originality, boldness, energy, and variety of character. To find a really original man living in an original and characteristic house, is as satisfactory as to find an eagle's nest built on the top of a mountain crag.

By illustrating villas in the Norman style, the Italian style, and the cottage villa in the Rural Gothic style, Downing helped to create a demand that architects and pattern-book publishers rushed to supply. As a consequence, the villa in a variety of picturesque architectural styles began to appear in all parts of the country.

In using the term "picturesque," Loudon, Downing, and Davis were repeating English aesthetic theory advanced by Uvedale Price in his *Essays on the Picturesque* (1794), wherein, according to Loudon, Price drew attention "to the beauty of irregularity in all country buildings, where the object aimed at is any thing beyond bare shelter and utility." Mid- to late-eighteenth-century theorists, most notably Edmund Burke, believed that visual delight could be divided into the Sublime and the Beautiful — the latter associated with rounded curves, smooth surfaces, delicacy, and proportion and the former involving vastness, wonder, surprise, and even terror. Price found this division insufficient and argued for a third classification that he called Picturesque, as in the case of a once-beautiful building in ruin that is now encrusted with plants and stained by weather so that "all trace of design are totally gone."

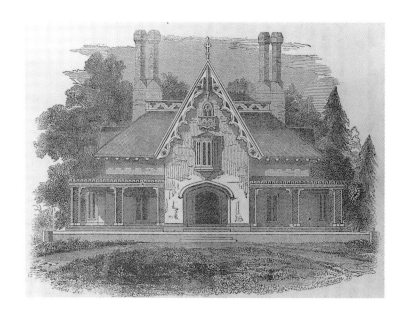

Alexander Jackson Davis designed this romantic villa in the Rural Gothic style for William Rotch of New Bedford, Massachusetts, and Downing published it in The Architecture of Country Houses, *remarking that "the character expressed by the exterior of this design is that of a man or family of domestic tastes, but with strong aspirations after something higher than social pleasures." (The Athenaeum of Philadelphia)*

Joseph Lee painted this view of Oak Knoll near Napa, California, in the 1860s. At the time of the painting, the owner was Robert B. Woodward, proprietor of a San Francisco amusement park. (The Fine Arts Museums of San Francisco, gift of Mrs. George E. Raum)

When the multimillionaire Andrew
M. Eastwick returned in 1850 to
Philadelphia from Russia, where he
had been building the St. Peters-
burg–Moscow Railway, he selected
the young architect Samuel Sloan
(1815–1884) to design a romantic
villa for him on the west bank of the
Schuylkill. The Norman-style Bar-
tram Hall—shown here from Sloan's
Model Architect—helped to launch
his career. (The Athenaeum of
Philadelphia)

But there may still remain an object which attracts
notice. Has it then no character when that of beauty
is departed? is it ugly? is it insipid? is it merely cu-
rious? Ask the painter, or the picturesque traveller;
they never abandon a ruin to the mere antiquary, till
none but an antiquary would observe it. Whatever
then has strong attractions as a visible object, must
have a character; and that which has strong attractions for the painter, and yet is neither grand nor
beautiful, is justly called picturesque.

The characteristics of "picturesque" architecture,
then, will be "the two opposite qualities of roughness and
of sudden variation, joined to that of irregularity...."

And since this description might equally be applied to a
building and its setting, Loudon argued that the landscape properly will dictate the appropriateness of certain
architectural styles, and "rude, rocky, hilly, and very
irregular surfaces" will "require the Castle Gothic."

Loudon's explanation of the picturesque may not have
rolled like a thunderclap across the Hudson Valley, but
it certainly fell on receptive ears. Of course literary al-
lusions to the Gothic had appeared in such eighteenth-
century novels as Horace Walpole's *The Castle of Otranto*,
Mrs. Radcliffe's *Mysteries of Udolpho*, and Matthew G.
Lewis's *The Monk*—all of which were known and read
by literate Americans. But in the works of Walter Scott,
The Lady of the Lake and the Waverly novels in particular,

Americans were swept up by the full flowering of romantic medievalism in which the picturesque qualities and emotional impact of Gothic architecture play an important role. By the 1830s the rugged banks of the Hudson were already being likened to those of the Rhine,

reinforcing the romantic medievalism Washington Irving's *Legend of Sleepy Hollow* had lent to the area, portraying Ichabod Crane and Brom Bones as competing knights for Katrina Van Tassel who lived in a "castle."

At Abbotsford — Walter Scott's own castellated country house near the ruined choirs of Melrose Abbey — the author played out his fantasies as laird of a border keep, and the house itself became a symbol of the picturesque and a place of literary pilgrimage. In 1817 the youthful Washington Irving visited the master of Abbotsford and later, when the time came to create his own house — Sunnyside — on the banks of the Hudson, he installed distinctive stepped gables said to originate with early New York Dutch buildings but which echo a similar detail at Abbotsford. James Fenimore Cooper likewise fell under the spell of Scott and popularized the comparison of the Hudson and the Rhine in his novel *The Heidenmauer* (1832); after visiting Abbotsford, he would crenelate Otsego Hall at Cooperstown.

It is against this philosophical, literary, and architectural background that the Hudson River villas, particularly those in the medieval styles, need to be viewed. Otherwise, such creations as the actor Edwin Forrest's Fonthill or J. J. Herrick's Ericstan make little sense at all. This is not to suggest these houses were universally praised. The architect William Ranlett remarked of Fonthill: "a wealthy actor is building himself a granite mansion on a conspicuous site upon the banks of the Hudson which looks as though the design had been copied from Macbeth's Castle, as exhibited on the stage." Even Downing's magazine *The Horticulturist* commented,

A proprietor on the lower part of the Hudson is building a stone castle, with all the towers clustered together; after the fashion of the old robber-strongholds on the Rhine. We trust he has no intention of levying tolls on the railroad that runs six times a day under his frowning battlements, or exacting booty from the rivercraft of all sizes forever floating by.

Ericstan, designed in 1855 by Alexander Jackson Davis in Tarrytown, survives only in his evocative watercolors and in photographs, but it must have been one of the most extraordinary essays in the medieval castellated style in America. Yet for all the success of his work at Montgomery Place and dozens of other significant public and private structures in several styles, Davis's most famous building remains the picturesque Gothic-style villa he designed in 1838–41 at Tarrytown, New York, as a summer retreat for the wealthy lawyer William Paulding

Otsego Hall, James Fenimore Cooper's house in Cooperstown, New York, was built by his father in the late eighteenth century and then extensively remodeled after the author returned from Europe in 1834. This daguerreotype, taken shortly before the house burned in 1853, shows Cooper's Gothicizing. (New York State Historical Society)

Fonthill, in Riverdale, New York, was erected by actor Edwin Forrest (1848–1852) and named for William Beckford's Fonthill Abbey near Bath, England. It is now part of Mount St. Vincent College. From A. A. Turner, Villas on the Hudson (New York, 1860). (Dornsife Collection of The Victorian Society in America at The Athenaeum of Philadelphia)

(1770–1854) and his son Philip Rhinelander Paulding (d.1864).

The Paulding family had ties to Tarrytown dating back to the seventeenth century; the elder Paulding had served in Congress, was a brigadier general during the War of 1812, and was twice elected mayor of New York City. James Kirk Paulding, William's brother, had joined with Washington Irving and his brothers to produce the *Salmagundi; or, the Whim-Whams and Opinions of Launcelot Langstaff, Esq. and Others* (New York, 1807–1808), a series of whimsical essays modeled on the *Spectator*. Wash-

ington Irving, who had taken refuge with the Pauldings at Tarrytown in 1798 during a yellow fever outbreak in New York, later became their neighbor. In 1835 he purchased a cottage from the Van Tassel family, which he remodeled into the present Sunnyside on the banks of the Hudson just south of the Paulding house.

Then called the Knoll, Paulding Manor, or Paulding Place, the Paulding house commands the east bank of

Few early-Victorian architectural drawings so evocatively capture the romantic picturesque villa as Alexander Jackson Davis's 1855 watercolor of the moonlit Ericstan, Tarrytown, New York. (Metropolitan Museum of Art, H. B. Dick Fund)

Designed for J. J. Herrick by Alexander Jackson Davis, Ericstan, shown here in a photolithograph made shortly after the house was completed, was demolished in 1944. From A. A. Turner, Villas on the Hudson *(New York, 1860). (Dornsife Collection of The Victorian Society in America at The Athenaeum of Philadelphia)*

the Hudson, just below the modern Tappan Zee Bridge, from which it may be seen on a clear day. It stands today as the premier surviving example of Davis's romantic, picturesque villas in the Hudson River Valley, reflecting in its two periods of building both his early and mature handling of the Gothic Revival style. Two years prior to the Paulding commission, Davis had begun putting together his *Rural Residences*, the second American book of architecture with colored plates (after Birch's *Country Seats*, which is more pictorial than architectural). *Rural Residences* was to be issued in six parts, but only two appeared because of the growing financial panic of 1837 that soon developed into a full-blown depression. *Rural*

Residences is heavily influenced by English books of picturesque architecture, including Loudon's *Encyclopedia*, of course, as well as Robert Lugar's *Villa Architecture* (London, 1828), John Papworth's *Rural Residences, consisting of a Series of Designs for Cottages, small villas, and other*

The extraordinary interior of Ericstan's fan-vaulted parlor illustrates the extent to which the picturesque medieval style was carried into the interior of Davis's Rhenish castles. (Avery Architectural Library, Columbia University)

ornamental Buildings (London, 1818 and 1832), and Francis Goodwin's *Domestic Architecture* (London, 1833–34, reissued as *Rural Architecture* in 1835).

With so few copies of Davis's ill-fated book sold, it could not have been particularly influential, and it is more likely that his designs that appeared in the popular publications of Andrew Jackson Downing were what helped to disseminate the appeal of houses set harmoniously within a natural landscape where irregularity of outline, variety of texture, and judiciously selected colors created a picturesque whole. Downing's publications made Davis the most popular architect of romantic country houses in America. Still, Davis's text and illustrations for *Rural Residences* tell us what *he* thought was important on the eve of the Lyndhurst commission. Rejecting such Greek-

temple country houses as Thomas Ustick Walter's Andalusia for "defects . . . not only in the style of the house but in the want of connection with its site," he called for "picturesque Cottages and Villas" such as could be found in England.

What emerged from Davis's fertile synthesis of English publications is first seen in the asymmetrical mass and irregular outline of Paulding's house. To the north it is anchored with a crenelated square tower; to the south it trails away in a low, graceful veranda that wraps around and shelters the drawing room with its French windows opening on the surrounding gardens and the view of the Hudson below. Centered in the façade is a projecting block with buttressed walls and a large tracery window over late medieval pointed arches that form the *porte-*

Early-nineteenth-century British architects published several books of picturesque designs such as this buff and brownstone Gothic-style house intended to harmonize with garden scenery, from Robert Lugar's Villa Architecture *(London, 1828). (Dornsife Collection of The Victorian Society in America at The Athenaeum of Philadelphia)*

cochère. Rising above this central feature are twin chimneys and the suggestion of a finial, which accentuate the verticality and irregularity of the outline, qualities that would be strengthened by Davis when he returned a quarter of a century later to extend the house.

The profession of architect was just emerging in America, and men like Davis in New York and Thomas Ustick Walter in Philadelphia struggled to convince clients to pay for the *design* itself — a service that had been provided by master builders such as Thomas Nevell and William Williams as part of the building costs or for a modest additional charge. Architects began to press for payment based on a percentage of the cost of the house, *and* they wanted to supervise the progress of the building

and be paid for the supervision. Davis later complained that Paulding didn't understand the importance of the architect's supervision. "The consequence was, that the mullions of the windows were made too small by nearly one half; the drip stones and copings incorrect and vulgar," he wrote.

Ironically, the first successful professional architect in America, Benjamin Henry Latrobe, had had a similar experience in 1799 when he attempted to introduce a vaguely Gothic house to Philadelphia. Sedgeley, a villa designed for William Crammond, and erected on the banks of the Schuylkill, presented the local house carpenters with the problem of having to execute molding profiles and other details that departed from conventional practice. Unfortunately, Latrobe was given no responsibility for overseeing the execution of his design. Unless the architect is engaged to "the furnishing of drawings for the *whole detail* as the building progresses," he later wrote,

the architect becomes responsible in reputation for all the whims, the blunders, many of them perhaps expensive, of the various mechanics who execute [the general design]. It is unfortunate for the profession that here the department of design & direction is not separate from that of execution, by which means, especially in the erection of Mr. Crammond's house on the Schuylkill I have been disgraced both by the

The original Paulding dining room of 1838, shown here in Davis's rendering that illustrates the wall painted to simulate stone, became the library when Lyndhurst was enlarged in the 1860s. (Metropolitan Museum of Art, A. J. Davis Collection, H. B. Dick Fund)

deformity & expense of some parts of the building, because, after giving the first general design, I had no further concern with it.

Walter and Davis had attempted to found an American Institution of Architects in 1836 to develop uniform standards for those who would style themselves architects and to educate clients about the differences between designer and builder. Unfortunately the new society foundered during the economic depression, and the present American Institute of Architects was not founded until 1857.

Lack of supervisory responsibility notwithstanding, Davis seemed happy with the overall result of the Paulding house. Downing, who visited during its construction, wrote Davis that he was "exceedingly pleased" with the result; "I think it does you great credit — indeed I have never seen anything to equal it, as I conceive it will be when finished." The New York merchant Philip Hone also gives us a contemporary reaction when he recorded in his diary a trip up the Hudson in 1841:

In the course of our drive we went to see Mr. Paulding's magnificent house, yet unfinished, on the bank below Tarrytown. It is an immense edifice of white or gray marble, resembling a baronial castle, or rather a Gothic monastery, with towers, turrets and trellises; archways, armories and airholes; peaked windows and pinnacled roofs, and many other fantastics too tedious to enumerate, the whole constituting an edifice of gigantic size, with no room in it; which if I mistake not, will one of the days be designated as 'Paulding's folly.'

Davis also provided Paulding with fifty furniture designs (at $1.00 each) much in the feel of Robert Conner's

Cabinet Makers' Assistant (New York, 1842) and more directly inspired by plates from Rudolph Ackermann's *Repository of Arts, Literature, Commerce, Manufactures, Fashions and Politics* (London, 1809–28). A few of the pieces based on those designs remain in the house, most notably chairs made for Paulding's "saloon"—now exhibited in

The extent of the Merritt additions to Lyndhurst are shown in this west front elevation and plan (c.1865) by Davis. (Metropolitan Museum of Art, A. J. Davis Collection, H. B. Dick Fund)

the vestibule together with a Davis-designed round table — and chairs made for the second-floor art gallery.

In 1864, George Merritt, a wealthy merchant from Troy, New York, who had patented an innovative railroad car spring and retired on the proceeds, acquired The Knoll from Paulding's heirs and renamed it Lyndhurst. It was he who invited Davis to return and enlarge the house — ultimately doubling it. If Philip Hone thought "Paulding's folly" large, one wonders what he would have thought of Merritt's Lyndhurst. Now a mature designer with most of his career behind him, Davis boldly added to the north a one-hundred-foot tower worthy of an English parish church. He then just as quickly dropped below the roofline of his original house for the dining room wing. Davis brilliantly solved the problem of extending the ground plan while balancing the mass of the original house by stepping these additions back from the original façade, adding substantially to the picturesque sense of recess and projection to match the complexity of the outline.

The Merritt occupancy of Lyndhurst proved to be relatively brief. The next owners, the financier Jay Gould and his heirs, were to bring the greatest public notoriety to the house. "Robber baron" Jay Gould (1836–1892) came from a modest farming family and paid for a rudimentary education at a local academy by blacksmithing and clerking at a store, ultimately setting himself up as a surveyor. A number of career shifts followed for this

West front of Lyndhurst today. *(Photograph by Jim Frank, Rye, New York)* ▶

East front of Lyndhurst today. *(Photograph by Jim Frank, Rye, New York)*

"undersized, keen-witted, unscrupulous young man" who, at the age of thirty-one, had amassed sufficient wealth to join with James Fisk in successfully challenging the Vanderbilt interests for control of the Erie Railroad. Leveraging the profits from fraudulently watered Erie stock — he converted construction bonds into unauthorized stock that he then sold — Gould acquired controlling interest in several western railroads that he manipulated to his personal benefit — acquiring in the process the du-

bious appellation "the most hated man in America."

In search of a summer house near New York City where his wife, Helen Day Miller Gould, and their six children would be secure from verbal abuse or physical attack, Jay Gould leased Lyndhurst in 1878 from Merritt's widow. Two years later he purchased the house and 550 acres for $250,000. Each day he journeyed down the Hudson to New York City in his steam yacht, *Atalanta*, to manage ever-widening financial interests. During these

The dining room added to Lyndhurst by Davis for George Merritt. (Photograph by Jim Frank, Rye, New York) ▶

George Merritt converted what was originally designed as the Pauldings' second-floor library to an art gallery, a use continued by Jay Gould. (Photograph by Jim Frank, Rye, New York)

early years at Lyndhurst, Gould acquired the New York *World*, the Western Union Telegraph Company, and control of New York's elevated railways. Lyndhurst pro-

The hall looking toward the drawing room shows the original painted decoration that simulates blocks of marble. (Photograph by Jim Frank, Rye, New York)

vided release from the pressure cooker of this empire; it became a family haven where he indulged his private passions: raising orchids and reading.

By all accounts these were happy years for the Goulds, and their eldest daughter, Helen, developed a particular fondness for the house and its site. In early 1889, however, Mrs. Gould suffered a series of strokes and died at the age of fifty-one, to be followed by her husband only three years later, dead at fifty-six of tuberculosis. Helen lived on at Lyndhurst, which she purchased from her father's estate. (Gould placed his fortune in trust and divided it equally among his children. As we shall see, this was not typical of such families.) Miss Gould presided as absolute mistress of Lyndhurst for nearly forty years, taking an active interest in the far-flung family empire now managed by her brothers and dispensing much of her income to various charities. But the story does not end here. In 1913 this middle-aged spinster unexpectedly married Finley J. Shepard, an employee of the Gould empire, and promptly began adopting orphans in place of the children she and her husband could not have. Lyndhurst was filled with children once again.

Following Helen Gould Shepard's death on the eve of World War II, her husband sold the house to Helen's younger sister, Anna, the dowager Duchesse de Talleyrand-Périgord, who had lived in France for most of her adult life. Lyndhurst had been her childhood home, and both sentiment and prudence dictated her return to America in 1939. Anna had first married the penniless Count Boni de Castellane — who squandered a substantial part of his wife's income before she divorced him for promiscuity, an act he repaid with a kiss-and-tell autobiography entitled *How I Discovered America* — and then the older and wealthier Duc de Talleyrand-Périgord. How the daughter of a self-made American millionaire became the wife of not one but two European aristocrats is a tale too long to recount here. Suffice it to say that in the late nineteenth century the exchange of comely daughters by *nouveau-riche* Americans for European titles had become a much-honored symbiosis that seems to have been mutually satisfying to the families of both parties, if not to the individual involved.

Now Anna, "the Duchesse," reigned over Lyndhurst as had her sister, spending half the year on the banks of the Hudson, the balance in France with her daughter and grandchildren. In ill health, she returned to France in the summer of 1961, where she died a few months later. Under her will Lyndhurst was to go to the National Trust for Historic Preservation, but in the last months

of her life Anna had attached five suspiciously conflicting codicils to the original document. Only after a protracted contest between the Trust and the Duchesse's heirs was Lyndhurst released to become a museum—shorn, unfortunately, of the $3,000,000 endowment the last of Jay Gould's surviving children had intended to support one of the great American country houses.

Montgomery Place and Lyndhurst may ultimately tell us as much about their architect as their owners. In the instance of Olana, the home of the Hudson River School painter Frederic Edwin Church, however, architect and client are fused. When asked if he had served as his own architect, Church replied, "Yes, I can say, as the good woman did about her turtle soup, 'I made it out of my head.'"

Like no other country house in America, Olana was conceived and executed as a true picturesque composition that blurs the already thin line between art and architecture and may even fit Burke's definition of the Sublime in its ability to surprise the viewer. Olana may also be

Photographic portrait of Jay Gould (1836–1892). (National Trust for Historic Preservation)

The Atalanta, Jay Gould's steam yacht. (National Trust for Historic Preservation)

Church's greatest composition, an extraordinary statement to make about a man who founded a reputation in the third quarter of the last century on such monumental paintings as *Niagara* (1857) and *The Heart of the Andes* (1859), which sold for $10,000, then the highest price ever paid for a landscape by a living American artist. Frederic Edwin Church (1826–1900) was born in Hartford, Connecticut. He began studying art while still in his teens and by 1844 had moved to Catskill, New York, where he worked for two years with the pioneer Hudson River School painter Thomas Cole. Church sold his first painting to a museum in 1846, established a studio in New York City the following year, and in 1860 — firmly established as a celebrated and prosperous artist — he married the beautiful Isabel Carnes. Shortly before the wedding, Church purchased a hillside farm at Hudson, New York, across the river from where he had lived while studying with Cole. A simple house — called Cozy Cottage — was erected for seasonal use from designs by Church's New York friend and contemporary Richard Morris Hunt. Hunt was the first American architect trained at the École des Beaux-Arts, Paris: we will encounter his mature work in the next chapter.

Each summer the Churches would journey up the Hudson to the farm, which was kept fully operational by a manager. According to Henry T. Tuckerman in *Book of the Artists, American Artist Life* (New York, 1867), "It is Church's habit to devote the summer to observation and reflection; then he gathers the materials, and thinks over the plan and scope of his pictures, seeking at the same time, by life in the open air . . . [to] lay up a stock of strength as well as ideas for work during the winter. That season he passes in the city, resolutely shut up several hours daily in his studio, concentrating his mind upon some long-contemplated task, to which his time and thoughts are given with rare and exclusive devotion."

Church had long coveted the summit above his farm, from which, according to an *Art Journal* article (1876), there

. . . is the grandest and most impressive view of the Catskill Mountains. In the deep valley flows the Hudson River between high and wooded banks. To the south it suddenly broadens to a width of two miles, forming a beautiful lake with picturesque shores. In the distance rise various mountain chains, including the Highlands at West Point, sixty miles away.

Or as Church put it a few years after purchasing the top of the hill in 1867, "About an hour this side of Albany is the Center of the World — I own it."

At this spot, Church proposed to erect a house worthy of the site, a house from which every feature of the changing panorama spread out in all directions across the Hudson and the mountains beyond might be captured. For this Richard Morris Hunt designed "A Country Villa" a fairly conventional, asymmetrical, brick Queen Anne–style house with a vaguely French square tower. But before construction could begin, the Churches set off for Europe and the Middle East, spending nearly six months touring the eastern Mediterranean with stops in Beirut, Jerusalem, Damascus, Cyprus, Rhodes, and Constantinople. The Churches were completely smitten by the

Southwest façade of Olana, the Hudson River villa of Frederic Edwin Church, erected in 1870–72 near the modern Rip Van Winkle Bridge south of Albany, New York. The name was chosen by Mrs. Church after an "old Latin name of a place in Persia, to which the artist's home bears resemblance in situation." (New York State Office of Parks, Recreation and Historic Preservation, Olana State Historic Site)

Frederic Church's Niagara (oil on canvas, 1857), his most famous painting, was widely exhibited both here and abroad during his lifetime. (Corcoran Gallery of Art, Washington, D.C.)

Mark Twain saw The Heart of the Andes (oil on canvas, 1859) in St. Louis and wrote to his brother that it leaves "your brain grasping and straining with futile efforts to take all the wonder in . . . and understand how such a miracle could have been conceived and executed by human brain and human hands. You will never get tired of looking at the picture. . . ." (Metropolitan Museum of Art)

exoticism of what they had seen; writing from Bavaria, where they rested for a month in 1868 after the return journey up the Danube from Constantinople and the Black Sea, Church declared, "I have got plenty of capital ideas and new ones about house building." In addition, the Churches acquired fifteen crates of "rugs — armour — stuffs — curiosities . . . Arab spears — beads from Jerusalem — stones from Petra and 10,000 other things."

Frederic E. Church, Twilight in Winter *(oil sketch, c. 1871), looking south over the Hudson from the site of Olana. (New York State Office of Parks, Recreation and Historic Preservation, Olana State Historic Site)*

Just how extensive Church's "capital ideas" proved to be is reflected in the changes from Hunt's earlier design, although the massing of the house that Mrs. Church eventually christened Olana ("the old Latin name of a place in Persia") is indebted to the original Hunt design. Ironically, the first change appears to have been in the choice of architects, for reasons that are not entirely clear. From what later transpired we know that Church intended to take an active hand in the design, and some historians have suggested Hunt was unwilling to accept a more passive role. (Church suggested that when he wrote, "A young architect is more painstaking and more tractable than an old and popular one.") Whatever the reason, Church turned to the English-born architect Calvert Vaux (1824–1895), who had come to the United States in the 1850s to work with Andrew Jackson Downing in Newburgh, New York, where he became an intimate of several Hudson River School artists.

Though Downing died tragically in 1852 when the steamboat *Henry Clay* burned while racing the *Armenia* on the Hudson River, Vaux remained in Newburgh. In 1857, he wrote in his book *Villas and Cottages* that architecture derives its "greatest glory" from association with sculpture and painting—a point of view likely to appeal to Church. By the time excavations began for the house in 1870, Vaux had established himself in New York in partnership with the landscape architect Frederick Law Olmsted, with whom he won the competition for Central Park. Simultaneously, Vaux maintained an architectural partnership with Frank Clarke Withers, and the earliest Olana drawings carry the Vaux, Withers, and Company stamp.

Church would overwhelm his architect with hundreds of sketches and letters confirming that he took a day-to-day interest in the form as well as the embellishment of Olana. It appears fairly certain from both the surviving drawings in Church's hand and his correspondence that Vaux did little more than convert the client's fertile concepts into acceptable construction documents. Church's later work at Olana without the assistance of an archi-

tect's trained hand resulted in some rather unfortunate structural flaws. Early in the project he apologized to a friend for being a tardy correspondent because,

1st I am building a house and am principally my own Architect. I give directions all day and draw plans and working drawings all night. 2nd I have my studio affairs outside and inside to attend to, 3rd I have a large farm to keep an eye on, 4th I have my family to take care of, 5th I have been away on business three or four times since you wrote, and 6th an infant daughter aged four days has engrossed a good deal of my time.

Sitting room, Olana, with Church's painting El Khasné, Petra (oil on canvas, 1874) hanging over the fireplace. The painting was a gift to Mrs. Church, and the sunlit stone of the ruins at Petra established the color scheme for this room, which was used primarily by the family. (The Friends of Olana)

Two of the three hundred surviving drawings for Olana by Church. "Sometimes the desire to build attacks a man like a fever—and at it he rushes," Church wrote. (New York State Office of Parks, Recreation and Historic Preservation, Olana State Historic Site)

The popularity of Middle Eastern–inspired design in the Victorian era was mostly confined to interior decoration in American residential architecture, and among the major houses that drew extensively on it for inspiration—such as P. T. Barnum's Iranistan and Samuel Colt's Armsmear—most do not survive, making Olana appear all the more exotic to modern eyes. Vaux's first partner, Andrew Jackson Downing, had commented favorably on "the Saracenic, or Moorish style" in his *A Treatise on the Theory and Practice of Landscape Gardening* (New York, 1841), calling it "rich in fanciful decoration," "striking and picturesque in its detail," and "worthy of the attention of the wealthy amateur." Vaux generally echoed this sentiment but felt it was primarily a *decorative* style and one too expensive for more than "isolated features" introduced for effect. Church admitted to the artist John Ferguson Weir,

> I hope to be in New York in a week or so—but a Feudal Castle which I am building—under the modest name of a dwelling house—absorbs all my time and attention. I am obliged to watch it so closely—for having undertaken to get my architecture from Persia where I have never been—nor any of my friends either—I am obliged to imagine Persian architecture—then embody it on paper and explain it to a lot of mechanics whose ideal of architecture is wrapped up in felicitous recollections of a successful brick school house or meeting house or jail. Still—I enjoy this being afloat on a vast ocean paddling along in the dreamy belief that I shall reach the desired port in due time.

Olana is unlike anything else to be found in America. Church's biographer characterizes it as "a Persianized amalgam of Italian villa, Gothic revival, Ruskinian poly-

Early design for Olana by Calvert Vaux, who later admitted that most of the credit for the house should go to the client, not to his architect. (New York State Office of Parks, Recreation and Historic Preservation, Olana State Historic Site)

chromy, and French mansard, with an East Indian shingle-style wing" — in other words, it defies stylistic classification. The house was erected of stone quarried on the site and polychrome brickwork: yellow, red, and black below a slate roof of gray, red, and pale green. It is this exotic and skillful mosaic of color and pattern rather than the open towers, Islamic arches, and balconies that prepares the first-time visitor for the brilliance of what is to come. Here landscape artist also became landscape architect. Olana is surrounded by three hundred acres of lawn, meadow, and woods — traversed by seven and a half miles of roads, all of which Church carefully planned. "I can make more and better landscapes in this way," he wrote, "than by tampering with canvas and paint in the studio."

For all its apparent bulk, Olana is not a large house; the main structure provides only four bedchambers and two baths. The reception rooms are domestic rather than palatial in scale, deriving their chief appeal from the views and decoration. In plan, all rooms of the original house

Iranistan, the country villa of showman Phineas T. Barnum near Bridgeport, Connecticut, was inspired by the Royal Pavilion in Brighton, England, and owes more to Indian than to Persian antecedents. Designed by Leopold Eidlitz, the house was completed in 1848 and destroyed by fire ten years later. This view appeared across the top of Barnum's letterhead. (The Athenaeum of Philadelphia)

ceiling, is the largest of the original rooms at Olana. The walls were painted maroon up to the sills of the high windows as a backdrop for the paintings; above the sills, they were painted the khaki hue the Victorians called drab. The author Grace King tells of dining there in the company of Mark Twain and the Churches in 1887, although she appears to have been oblivious to the European paintings massed around her in their gilt frames. "The dining room is a great square space. The only light comes through high gothic [*sic*] arched windows at one end — the soft northern light. I noticed a magnificent carved Florentine chest on one side — a table inlaid with mother-of-pearl — gorgeous old persian rugs everywhere.

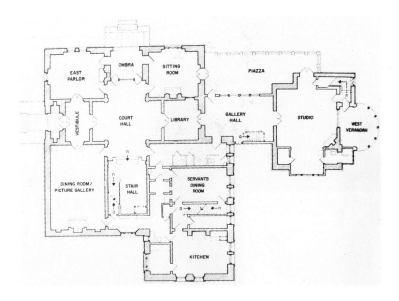

Ground floor plan of Olana. The studio and its connecting gallery were added by Church in 1888 when he decided to relinquish his New York City studio. (The Friends of Olana)

open off the court hall, with its spellbinding view over the Hudson through the Moorish-arched "ombra," which also served the Churches as a conservatory for plants. Opposite the ombra, the grand stairway — rising from a stage elevated four steps above the court hall floor — is visually softened and separated by portières of a Middle Eastern carpet pattern. This central space serves the same role as the living hall commonly found in American Queen Anne–style houses of the period: arriving guests would be greeted here and directed to the east parlor (normally used for entertaining), the sitting room (more intimate and used by the family), the library, or the dining room/picture gallery.

Because Church intended it to serve double duty, the dining room/picture gallery, with its seventeen-foot-high

The court hall as it appeared c. 1890, when Church had the entire house photographed. This view, with the ombra behind the photographer, looks toward the dining room door. (The Friends of Olana)

The dinner was very elaborate, beautifully served." Under the four windows on the north wall is an exotic brass fireplace surround designed by Church for the room.

The basic structure was sufficiently completed by 1872 for the Churches to occupy the upper floor while the ground level was being decorated. In decorating the interior, Church seems to have been greatly influenced by Jules Bourgoin's *Les Arts Arabes* (Paris, 1868), a copy

The court hall at Olana is the central space off which open all the other ground-floor rooms; it is also the most exotically furnished, with armor, vases, hangings, carpets, and brassware from Persia, Turkey, India, China, and Japan—all of which came under the vague heading of "oriental" in the Victorian age. (The Friends of Olana)

of which he owned, and from which he derived the Islamic stencil patterns used to decorate the doors in reflective metallic paints. Here too he could unleash the artist's palette, dipping his brush deeply into the wonderful tertiary colors of the later nineteenth century: plum, peacock blue, citron, terra cotta, russet, and claret—each taken up in the court hall and carried off to enrich the other rooms in turn. The pattern is Islamic,

the colors High Victorian, the inspiration pure Church, the whole a visual delight.

Both the Churches were plagued with ill health; Mrs. Church gradually went blind, and by 1876 Frederic Church was suffering from the "inflammatory rheumatism" that caused him to curtail painting; around 1880 he ceased serious work. Unable to endure New York winters, he began spending the colder months in Mexico,

Church intended the dining room to serve double duty as a picture gallery for his collection of Old Master paintings, many of which he retouched himself and most of which he purchased in Rome, mainly for decoration. "The highest price I have paid for one is $30, the lowest one dollar," he admitted in 1868. The dining room was to be an "old room—with old furniture and old pictures—everything toned down to 400 years back." (The Friends of Olana)

The east parlor occupies the ground floor of the southeast tower and contains several of Church's own paintings as well as Thomas Cole's Solitary Lake, New Hampshire. The stenciled doors were inspired by patterns from Jules Bourgoin's Les Arts Arabes *(Paris, 1868). (The Friends of Olana)*

The ombra frames the most dramatic view to the Hudson River, five hundred feet below. "As I looked from its broad veranda one beautiful sunshiny morning the scene that spread before me filled me with regret that I had the soul of an artist without the power to wield the brush," wrote one visitor. "It seemed the spot of all others to lend inspiration . . ." (The World, New York, July 21, 1889). *(The Friends of Olana)*

returning to Olana or to Lake Millinocket, Maine, in the spring.

Wishing to relinquish his New York studio, Church launched one last project at Olana in 1888, construction of a studio wing—actually a tower connected by a gallery—thrusting to the west off the library and projecting out over the hillside as it falls away to the Hudson below. In the building of this wing, he dispensed totally with professional architects. Church admitted to the sculptor Erastus Dow Palmer in a letter of September 11, "I am of course very busy superintending the New Studio. It takes a deal of time and no little study to keep so many men at work advantageously—As I have no regularly drawn plans I have to explain every detail. It is not a little difficult I find to keep the work going economically when none of the men really know what is coming next."

Church added the studio in 1888–89, serving as his own architect. He complained, "my old carpenter makes so many mistakes that I dared not leave home for a single day." (The Friends of Olana)

The studio was to be little used. Church struggled with his arthritis, and even taught himself to paint with his left hand. But more than physical disability stood between the master of Olana and the artistic world where once he had been hailed for producing, in John Ruskin's words, "an entirely new and higher view both of American nature and art." Artistic currents changed direction in the last quarter of the nineteenth century, and critics began to ridicule the romantic worldview of the Hudson River School painters. Concerning the paintings submitted to the Centennial Exhibition of 1876 in Philadelphia by Church's contemporary Albert Bierstadt, one reviewer wrote, they "lapse into sensational and meretricious effects, and a loss of true artistic aim. They are vast illustrations of scenery, carelessly and crudely executed, and we fail to discover in them the merits which rendered his earlier works conspicuous." The very year that Church abandoned New York City and began construction of his studio at Olana, Clarence Cook published *Art and Artists of Our Time*, in which most of the Hudson River School artists of the previous generation were passed over with minor mention. Church is dismissed for having "made himself a national reputation by a succession of pictures that are rather to be praised as records of famous places than as works of art in the higher sense."

Mrs. Church died in the spring of 1899, and Frederic Church spent the following winter in Mexico. But for him the Mexican sun no longer had restorative powers; he returned to New York City in March of 1900 and died at the home of his patron, William H. Osborn, on April 7. The Metropolitan Museum of Art mounted a memorial exhibition, yet one of the obituary notices remarked that "the fact that he was still alive has been almost forgotten by present day artists." As for Olana, it was inherited by the artist's son, Louis, who lived there until his death in 1943, and then by Louis's widow, who lived there until 1964. Filled with sketches and paintings, preserved as a shrine to the genius of Frederic Church, whose work is once again ascendant, the property remains much as it was in 1900 and is now owned and kept open to the public by the State of New York.

5

*T*HE *L*AST *G*REAT *C*OUNTRY *H*OUSES

In the decades prior to World War I, colossal riches poured from American mines, wells, and mills; great fortunes arose out of the needs of the rapidly expanding American people for food, housing, and transport. Taxes were low or nonexistent, servants plentiful and cheap. So much of this wealth found its way into the construction of substantial residences that the editors of *Artistic Houses* could boast in 1883, "The domestic architecture of no nation in the world can show trophies more original, affluent, or admirable" than those of America.

Often these trophies took the form of suburban palaces located near major metropolitan areas and based architecturally on British and European country houses, such as architect Horace Trumbauer's Whitemarsh Hall (1916–17), erected for the millionaire financier Edward T. Stotesbury in Chestnut Hill, Pennsylvania, or McKim, Mead & White's overblown version of Washington's

Mount Vernon designed for James L. Breese in Southampton, Long Island (1906). Wealthy patrons also commissioned vacation houses, such as the summer season "cottages" of Newport, Rhode Island, or winter retreats like oil magnate and Florida promoter Henry Morrison Flagler's Whitehall (1901) in Palm Beach, harvester manufacturer James Deering's Vizcaya (1914–16) in Miami, and circus owner John Ringling's Venetian *palazzo* Ca'd'Zan in Sarasota.

As a general rule, these suburban and holiday estates of the rich and famous should not be called country houses, no matter how architecturally rooted in the past or conspicuously extravagant. They rarely served as the "seat" of a family and certainly they were not reflective of the wealth and power derived from the land. Often used for only brief periods during the year, they owe more to the romantic villas of those halcyon days before

Philadelphia architect Horace Trumbauer designed the 147-room Whitemarsh Hall for Mr. and Mrs. Edward T. Stotesbury, 1916–17. Erected on four hundred acres in the suburban community of Chestnut Hill, Pennsylvania, the house and its gardens have been replaced by dozens of tract houses. (The Athenaeum of Philadelphia)

Henry Morrison Flagler built Whitehall (1901) in Palm Beach, Florida, as a wedding present for his third wife. Designed for a six-acre lot on Lake Worth by John M. Carrère and Thomas Hastings, the house was described by the New York Herald as "more wonderful than any palace in Europe, grander and more magnificent than any other private dwelling in the world." (Whitehall, the Henry Morrison Flagler Museum) ▶

America came of age—when men sought to escape the city and live in houses that expressed to the world their "taste and elegance"—but lack the romantic villa's carefully reasoned philosophical link between man, house, and nature. For most of these urban-centered owners, association with the land was incidental.

Designed by Paul Chalfin and F. Burrall Hoffman, Jr., Vizcaya (completed in 1916) dominates a ten-acre site on Biscayne Bay in Miami, Florida. The house is owned by Dade County and is operated as a house museum. (Vizcaya Museum and Gardens)

In 1912 circus impresario John Ringling and his wife, Mabel, acquired a thirty-eight-acre tract of land on Sarasota Bay, Florida. Several years later the Ringlings moved the frame house they had occupied for occasional winter vacations and erected on the site the Venetian-inspired Ca'd'Zan (House of John), designed by Dwight James Baum. It was completed in time for Christmas, 1926. After Ringling made Sarasota the winter quarters for his circus at the end of the 1927 season, the Ringlings occupied the house for two or three months each year. (John and Mabel Ringling Museum of Art)

Ironically, one of the best examples of a true country house dating from the early twentieth century is actually a ranch. As a general rule, ranches did not generate country houses, although several vernacular ranch houses—like their eastern farm-house cousins—have survived. Such an example from the Southwest is the unpretentious, plastered adobe and whitewashed de la Guerra House in Santa Barbara, California. It was erected in 1819–26 by the wealthy landowner Captain José Antonio de la Guerra, a mover and shaker in the province whose vast herds of cattle ranged over 200,000 acres. Other examples include the Los Cerritos ranch house, built by the New Englander Jonathan Temple in the California Monterey style, and the Petaluma ranch

house, once the center of a 66,000-acre spread north of San Francisco, both now open to the public as museums.

One of the most famous of the early ranch houses, unfortunately now gone, evolved from the simple frame shelter erected by Richard King (1824–1885) shortly after he purchased in 1853 three and a half square Spanish leagues (15,500 acres) of the Rincón de Santa Gertrudis where Santa Gertrudis Creek flows into Baffin Bay, forty-five miles below Corpus Christi, Texas.

The son of Irish immigrants, King began his career as a cabin boy and gradually worked himself up to pilot on the Gulf Coast rivers and bays between Mobile and the Rio Grande. At the conclusion of the Mexican War, King began his own riverboat company in 1849 with a

The de la Guerra House in Santa Barbara, California, shown here in a late-nineteenth-century photograph, *is actually a* casa de pueblo—*a house in town—rather than a true* hacienda, *or* casa de campo, *which would be associated with a farm or ranch, although architecturally there is little difference; the patio is surrounded on three sides by a* corredor (veranda). *(Santa Barbara Historical Society)*

Rancho Los Cerritos, erected by New Englander Jonathan Temple in 1844, commanded an estate of 27,000 acres on which he raised cattle for the hides and tallow trade. After Temple sold the property in 1866, the rancho was converted to sheep raising. The red tile roof was installed in this century when the house was remodeled in the "Mission Revival" style. (Rancho Los Cerritos Historic Site)

three-year-old war-surplus steamboat purchased for only $750 — it had cost the government $14,000 — because a cholera epidemic kept bidders away from the auction. The new shipping company prospered, and King began to invest in range land. He married, built the ranch house, which after the Civil War would acquire a second floor, and began to raise a family. During the Civil War, King realized a fortune moving southern cotton into Mexico, which gave him hard currency to purchase more land in the lean days of Reconstruction. At the time of his death he owned 614,000 acres (nearly 1,000 square miles) on which, as nearly as the appraisers of his estate could determine, grazed 40,000 head of cattle, 6,600 horses, and 12,000 sheep and goats.

During their marriage and after her husband's death, Mrs. King opposed replacing the original ranch house, which over the years had grown through additions. (Her

The Rancho Santa Gertrudis, designed by San Antonio architect Carleton W. Adams, was erected on the site of the original King ranch house. Today it is used as a guest house for members of the King-Kleberg family and visitors to the King Ranch headquarters. (King Ranch Archives)▶

The original Anglo-style ranch house at Santa Gertrudis, like Topsy in Uncle Tom's Cabin, *just "growed" to meet the increasing demands of the King family. It burned to the ground on January 4, 1912. (King Ranch Archives)*

Mariano Guadalupe Vallejo acquired his 66,000-acre Petaluma, California, ranch in 1834 when he was twenty-seven years old. Two years later he began to erect this adobe house for himself in the Spanish/Mexican patio layout (originally forming an open square) with overhanging eaves and balconies. (State of California Department of Parks and Recreation, photograph by Larry Costa)

opposition was not due to any hesitancy to display her position as one of the wealthiest Texans, for in 1893 she erected an ornate mansion in Corpus Christi.) Early on the morning of January 4, 1912, however, the ranch house burned to the ground, torched by a deranged gardener. Mrs. King's son-in-law and ranch manager, Robert Kleberg, set about building a proper house as "a monument to Mrs. King's hospitality." She is reported to have said that he could build anything he wanted so long as "anybody could walk in *in boots*."

The *casa grande* at Rancho Santa Gertrudis was erected on the ranch house site and turned out to be, in the words of one ranch historian, a mixture of "Mexican, Moorish and California Mission, of Long Island and Wild Horse Desert. . . ." The architect was Carleton W. Adams of San Antonio, and the interiors were executed by Tiffany in a restrained decor best described as "Southwest Mission," the stained-glass tower windows notwithstanding.

Rancho Santa Gertrudis can rightfully claim to be a country house, albeit with a wonderfully eclectic American flavor: it was the nerve center of a vast landed estate and symbolic of the wealth and power derived from that land. Today the house serves as the headquarters for the far-flung King Ranch empire.

Rare as true country houses from the late nineteenth and early twentieth centuries are, two attempts to establish country houses on vast landed estates stand out: George Washington Vanderbilt's Biltmore and William Randolph Hearst's San Simeon. Unlike the great plantation houses of the pre–Civil War South, neither of these

is (or could be in a post-industrial age) a product of the land on which they were built. They reflect wealth and power derived elsewhere. Yet both Vanderbilt and Hearst established emotional ties to the land on which they erected their houses; both sought to create working estates to emulate the pre-industrial relationship between land and house; both ultimately were doomed to fail.

George Washington Vanderbilt and William Randolph Hearst were born a few months apart at the height

The new house was designed around a central courtyard and fountain. (King Ranch Archives)

Departing from its typical flamboyant style, the Tiffany Studio designed this "Southwest Mission" interior for the new house at Santa Gertrudis. Mrs. King had directed that the house be decorated so that anyone there could be comfortable "in boots." (King Ranch Archives)

of the American Civil War to families of great wealth — wealth derived in best Victorian fashion from the control of railroads, real estate, and gold, silver, and copper mines. Separated by a continent and by a worldview no less wide, these two men created vastly different estates that when measured by sheer size, cost, and brilliance must be judged the apogee of the American country house.

Different as they are stylistically, the resulting houses — Vanderbilt's Biltmore in the mountains of North Carolina and Hearst's San Simeon overlooking the Pacific Ocean — reflect the age in which their owners came to maturity. They are more than the extravagant expressions of "robber baron" megalomania; both echo the vibrancy, confidence, and industrial prowess of America in the decades bracketing 1900, the age of the self-proclaimed "American Renaissance," the age when the United States emerged as a new colossus to rival Europe.

Nor could Vanderbilt and Hearst have brought forth these houses without astute collaborators: at Biltmore, Frederick Law Olmsted, the landscape architect largely responsible for New York's Central Park, and Richard Morris Hunt, the first American architect trained at the École des Beaux-Arts in Paris; and at San Simeon, Julia Morgan, the most famous female architect in American history and the first woman to be admitted to the École in Paris. Neither Vanderbilt nor Hearst initially planned to create the largest and most expensive country houses in America. Both thought first in terms of modest retreats, but at some unrecorded point, Vanderbilt's frame house and Hearst's bungalow were transformed into palaces worthy of a dukedom.

Whether it was the owners or the architects who first suggested enlarging the scope of the projects will probably never be known. Most likely it was a mutual drift, with artist sketching ever-larger potentials. "It was the artistic community that elevated the sights of the period," argues one historian. "The artistic community announced that America was the unique synthesis. It proclaimed that a new society based on science, industry, commerce, rational order, democracy, and the great energy of the people had been forged and was the legitimate heir to the concept of the Renaissance." And were not America's men of wealth like the merchant princes of Italy and France, were not her artists the new Bramante and Cellini, ready to serve these American Medici with appropriated architecture and decoration? Declared the architect Stanford White, "In the past, dominant nations had always plundered works of art from their predecessors; . . . America was taking a leading place among nations and had, therefore, the right to obtain art wherever she could." Both Vanderbilt and Hearst heartily subscribed to this rationale.

There is a proverb to the effect that the true test of a successful family comes in the third generation. George Washington Vanderbilt (1862–1914), the youngest of four sons born to William Henry Vanderbilt and his wife, Maria Louisa Kissam, daughter of a Brooklyn clergyman, was also the grandson of patriarch Cornelius Vanderbilt, founder of the family fortune. Young George Vanderbilt hardly knew his grandfather, who died in 1877 leaving most of his $100 million to George's father. (William Henry Vanderbilt is unfortunately remembered chiefly for a remark made to a Chicago reporter who asked if the passenger service on Vanderbilt's New York Central railroad wasn't provided for the public benefit. *The public be damned!*" Vanderbilt is quoted as saying. "What does the public care for the railroads except to get as much out of them for as small a consideration as possible! I don't take any stock in this working for anybody's good

*T*he library of Santa Gertrudis, photographed shortly after the house was furnished. (King Ranch Archives)

but our own, because we are not. When we make a move, we do it because it is our interest to do so. . . .")

When George Washington Vanderbilt was seventeen years old, his father decided to erect houses for himself and his two married daughters at 640 Fifth Avenue in New York City. They were designed by Charles B. Atwood and decorated by the ultra-fashionable New York firm Herter Brothers. William H. Vanderbilt's own house, estimated to have cost $3 million to build and furnish, turned out to be a late incarnation of the popular, formal mid-Victorian "Roman Renaissance" revival style. The restrained, men's club exterior gave little hint of the exotic decorations that live on long after their destruction in a lavish set of folios entitled *Mr. Vanderbilt's House and Collection*, which William H. Vanderbilt had published, as well as in the more widely distributed *Artistic Houses* (1883). A somewhat breathless description of the drawing room from the latter book gives a sense of the en-

The Fifth Avenue houses erected by William H. Vanderbilt for himself and his married daughters, 1879–81, described by Edward Strahan as ". . . the image of a typical American residence, seized at the moment when the nation began to have a taste of its own, an architecture, a connoisseurship, and a choice in the appliances of luxury, society, culture." George Washington Vanderbilt inherited life use of his father's house, but it passed out of his estate when he failed to produce a male heir. (The Athenaeum of Philadelphia)

vironment in which the teenage George Washington Vanderbilt was raised:

> The effect is gorgeous in the extreme: everything sparkles and flashes with gold and color — with mother-of-pearl, with marbles, with jewel-effects in glass — and almost every surface is covered, one might say weighted, with ornament: the walls, with carnation-red velvet, showing profusion of gilt *applique* work, which represents conventional [abstracted] trees whose flowers are made of jewels, and from whose branches hang festoons of gold-thread among which butterflies disport themselves. . . .

Only Oscar Wilde is missing.

As the youngest child of a large family — his eldest brother, Cornelius II, born in 1843, was nearly an adult when he was born in 1862 — George Washington Vanderbilt may well have been allowed to indulge his interest in art, architecture, interior decoration, and literature. His nearest siblings were girls, and there were already several sons tending to the flourishing family businesses. Frederick Law Olmsted found Vanderbilt "a delicate, refined and bookish man; with considerable humor, but shrewd, sharp, exacting and resolute in matters of business."

Upon his father's death in 1885, the twenty-three-year-old aesthete inherited life rights to the house and collections at 640 Fifth Avenue and $10 million — a substantial sum, though considerably less than the $67 million and $65 million that went to elder brothers Cornelius and William, who had followed their grandfather and father into the family businesses. He continued to share the Fifth Avenue mansion with his mother while dabbling in philanthropy; he financed a free public library, pur-

chased land for Columbia University, and erected an art gallery.

In the mid-1880s, George Vanderbilt and his mother visited Asheville, North Carolina, whose climate was reputed to be among the healthiest in North America: temperate but invigorating with long springs, mild winters, and summers with temperatures in the seventies. While out horseback riding, Vanderbilt came upon a rise overlooking the French Broad River. Here, he thought, would be a superb location for a house. Anonymously, he purchased about two thousand acres from the local hardscrabble farmers with the intention of erecting a wood-frame house where he and his mother could escape the cold New York winters.

Having acquired this parcel of land, Vanderbilt asked the most famous American landscape architect, Frederick Law Olmsted (1822–1903), to examine it to determine how, in Olmsted's words, he might "turn the larger part of the property to good account, as a matter of business, in a manner that would allow him to take some pleasure in its management and that would make the scenery and the advantages for a pleasant out-of-doors life not less agreeable than at present." The Vanderbilt and Olmsted families had known each other since the 1850s, when Frederick Law Olmsted had been farming at South Side on Staten Island. In 1858 Olmsted was appointed architect-in-chief of Central Park, and during the Civil War he served as executive secretary of the United States Sanitary Commission. By the late 1860s he had become a leading advocate for environmental planning and design. When asked to visit Asheville, Olmsted was already employed by George Vanderbilt on several projects, including landscaping the lot at the Vanderbilt mausoleum on Staten Island.

Olmsted found the land that Vanderbilt had pur-

A detail of the drawing room at
640 Fifth Avenue as decorated by
the Herter Brothers at a cost of
$800,000, illustrated in Edward
Strahan, Mr. Vanderbilt's House
and Collection *(New York, 1883).*
(The Athenaeum of Philadelphia)

Oil portrait of George Washington
Vanderbilt *(1862–1914) by John
Singer Sargent (1856–1925).*
(Biltmore Collection)

George Washington Vanderbilt brought John Singer Sargent to Biltmore in the spring of 1895 to paint portraits of Richard Morris Hunt and Frederick Law Olmsted to hang in the house, where they still may be seen. Hunt is posed on the terrace beside a marble wellhead in front of the spiral staircase. (Hunt's friend Joseph Choate called it "a ghastly thing, exhibiting in most glaring way the dreadful disease of which he was dying.") (Biltmore Collection)

In Sargent's portrait of Frederick Law Olmsted, the landscape architect is surrounded by the laurel, rhododendron, and dogwood that abound at Biltmore. Like Richard Morris Hunt, Olmsted was at the end of his career; the Biltmore house and gardens remain one of their most enduring monuments. (Biltmore Collection)

chased unpromising. The area had been overfarmed for generations, and the soil was exhausted; the surviving trees were inconsequential. In addition, he thought the entire Asheville region "generally poor and vagabondish." Only if Vanderbilt would adopt a planned environment—along the lines of aristocratic English and European estates—did the land possess potential. Olmsted particularly recommended making over most of the land into a forest, ". . . mainly with a view to crops of timber." He wrote to Vanderbilt:

> That would be a suitable and dignified business for you to engage in; it would, in the long run, be probably a fair investment of capital and it would be of great value to the country to have a thoroughly well organized and systematically conducted attempt in forestry made on a large scale. My advice would be to make a small park into which to look from your house; make a small pleasure ground and garden, farm your river bottom chiefly to keep and fatten live stock with a view to manure; and make the rest a forest, improving the existing woods and planting the old fields.

This concept of forestry, common enough in older cultures where timber land commands a premium, did not exist in America; rapacious exploitation of natural resources was the norm on a continent so bountifully endowed with virgin stands of wood. By the end of the nineteenth century, however, as eastern forests were depleted and those of the West threatened, a few farsighted naturalists like Olmsted called attention to the folly of this practice and encouraged both the conservation of surviving forests and the replenishment of once heavily timbered areas. Freed by his client's wealth from the immediate requirement to show a profit, Olmsted found

in this North Carolina plateau the perfect proving ground to establish forest management in America on a vast scale.

Vanderbilt ultimately assembled a duchy of 125,000 acres (nearly 200 square miles) at ever-increasing prices as the cagy Scotch-Irish who inhabited the region got wind of what was happening. (One farmer with nine acres in the middle of the projected estate resisted, claiming that he had "no objection to George Vanderbilt as a neighbor," but he too eventually sold out.) To manage the forest-to-be, Olmsted recommended that Vanderbilt hire a forester and in 1891 suggested young Gifford Pinchot (1865–1946), to whom Vanderbilt, only a few years his senior, took a liking.

Today the title "forester" probably calls to mind uniformed park rangers policing tourists' camp fires. This image hardly fits Gifford Pinchot. Born in Simsbury, Connecticut, to wealthy parents of French extraction, Pinchot studied at Yale and then at the École Nationale Forestière at Nancy in France. He was determined on a life in forestry, a career that did not even exist in America of the 1880s. While abroad, he met the leading European authority, Sir Dietrich Brandis, who warned him that there was no future for such a career in America "until some State or large individual owner makes the experiment and proves . . . that forest management will pay." George Vanderbilt and Frederick Law Olmsted made that experiment.

Coolly classical Marble House (completed in 1892), Newport, Rhode Island, was designed by Richard Morris Hunt for William K. Vanderbilt and is based in part on the garden façade of the Petit Trianon at Versailles. The interior, according to one observer, "erupts with unrestrained hedonism" in its use of gold leaf, bronze, and richly veined marbles. (The Preservation Society of Newport, Richard Cheek, photographer)

The hiring of Pinchot as first forester at Biltmore established Pinchot's career. He went on to become chief of the United States Forest Service, professor of forestry at Yale, and two-term governor of Pennsylvania. When he left Vanderbilt's employ in 1895, he recommended as his successor Carl Alwin Schenck, who two years later

founded the Biltmore School of Forestry, a pioneer American center for the training of scientific foresters. Following George Washington Vanderbilt's death in 1914, his widow donated 100,000 acres to the American people, forming the nucleus of Pisgah National Forest.

Of course, all this was in the future as Vanderbilt looked across the French Broad River to distant Mount Pisgah for the first time. His thoughts were on a house to command that view, a house that he would eventually

call Biltmore from *Bildt*, the Dutch town from which his paternal ancestors had come, and *more*, an Old English word for uplands. His choice of Richard Morris Hunt

The Breakers (completed in 1895), Newport, Rhode Island, designed by Richard Morris Hunt for Cornelius Vanderbilt II, may be the most palatial American mansion of the late nineteenth century. It is based on Renaissance merchants' palaces in Genoa. (The Preservation Society of Newport, Richard Cheek, photographer)

The Breakers dining room rises two full stories and is embellished with red alabaster columns, bronze Corinthian capitals, and elaborate gilded cornices. *(The Preservation Society of Newport, Richard Cheek, photographer)*

The main façade of Biltmore looks east across a four-acre esplanade with reflecting pool. Visitors enter this immaculately groomed area from the winding drive through the woods that Olmsted designed to hide the house until the last moment. (Biltmore Collection) ▶

Construction of Biltmore was systematically recorded by a local Asheville photographer hired by Vanderbilt. Shown here are the main entrance and staircase tower (1895), the billiard room and carriage porch (1893), and the roof being framed (1894). During this period Olmsted wrote to his partners that Biltmore is "the most distinguished private place, not only of America, but of the world . . ." then under construction. The limestone of which the house is built had to be hauled six hundred miles from Indiana. (Biltmore Collection)

(1818–1895) as architect would have surprised no one. Hunt had been the favorite architect of the Vanderbilt family for at least a decade, having executed houses at Oakdale, Long Island, and at 660 Fifth Avenue, New York City; he designed and supervised the construction of Marble House in Newport, Rhode Island, for George Vanderbilt's older brother, William K. Vanderbilt, at the

same time as Biltmore. For George Washington Vanderbilt himself, Hunt (collaborating with Olmsted) had designed the Vanderbilt mausoleum on Staten Island and remodeled a house at 9 West Fifty-third Street, New York City. And shortly after the completion of Biltmore, Vanderbilt had Hunt alter his father's mansion at 640 Fifth Avenue in New York City. Cornelius Vanderbilt II, George Vanderbilt's oldest brother, would cap Hunt's service to the family with The Breakers in Newport.

Fate placed the talented Richard Morris Hunt in position to take full advantage of the social insecurities of second- and third-generation American families of wealth. During the years Americans were forging a mod-

ern industrial nation, Hunt was in France studying art and architecture. His father, a prosperous New England congressman, died when Richard was a small child, and his mother moved the family to Europe. Opting for a career in architecture, he entered the studio of the French architect Hector Martin Lefuel and enrolled in the École des Beaux-Arts, Paris, where he became thoroughly imbued with historical French architectural styles. In the fall of 1855 he returned to the United States, writing to his mother,

It has been represented to me, that America was not ready for the fine arts, but I think they are mistaken.

Aerial view of Biltmore. (Biltmore Collection)

View from the tapestry gallery log-
gia, looking southwest across the
estate. Biltmore would eventually
command 125,000 acres. (Biltmore
Collection)

There is no place in the world where they are more needed, or where they should be more encouraged. Why, there are more luxurious houses put up in New York than in Paris! At any rate the desire is evinced and the money spent and if the object is not attained it is the fault of the architects. . . . There are no greater fools in America than in any other part of the world: the only thing is that the professional man with us has got to make his own standing.

To his contemporaries, Hunt appeared to specialize in "decorating the . . . privacies of the Vanderbilts and Goelets, the Marquands and Astors, the Belmonts and . . . Gerrys." Certainly his marriage to socially prominent Catharine Clinton Howland did not hurt his career, but the secret of his success was his brilliance as a designer of buildings in traditional European styles and an ability to sense what his wealthy clients wanted. "The first thing you've got to remember," he wrote to his son, "is that it's your clients' money you're spending. Your business is to get the best result you can, following their wishes. If they want you to build a house upside down, standing on its chimney, it's up to you to do it."

The house that Richard Morris Hunt designed for the Biltmore estate is inspired by the late-Gothic, early-Renaissance chateaux of Chambord, Chenonceaux, and Blois in France, a style Hunt first used for the large New York town house (1878–82) he designed for George Vanderbilt's brother, William K. Vanderbilt. At Biltmore, however, Hunt could freely indulge his architectural fantasies by erecting a chateau in appropriate country surroundings rather than on a cramped city lot — and do so virtually without economic limits. Hunt's biographer believes that the architect was the one who encouraged Vanderbilt to "build on a scale commensurate with the size of the holdings and the natural features of the prop-

erty." Indeed, as the house neared completion, Hunt would write to his wife, "the mountains are just the right size for the chateau!"

In 1889 Vanderbilt and Mr. and Mrs. Hunt made a whirlwind trip to Europe looking at chateaux and purchasing art and architectural elements to incorporate into the house. They would later visit the Chicago World's Fair and order much of the furniture for Biltmore from the London cabinetmakers Edwards & Roberts, who exhibited there.

During the summer of 1889, the house was staked out and scaffolds erected to the height of various proposed windows to check the views. Work at the site began late that year and was in full swing by the spring of 1890, employing several hundred workmen and a brick kiln producing 32,000 bricks each day. A three-mile-long railway spur was constructed at a cost of $77,500 to bring in the Indiana limestone that was to be the principal building material for the house. (The first train to use this newly completed track brought Vanderbilt's private railway car right to the esplanade where the house was to be erected.)

In spite of its size — ultimately 255 rooms — Biltmore came out of the ground quickly. The "downstairs" parts of the building — kitchens, swimming pool, store and furnace rooms — were completed in 1892, the second story in 1893, and the upper levels and roof structure by 1894. By the end of 1895 Biltmore was sufficiently complete for its owner to give a family Christmas party. One by

The site at the edge of a steep slope is apparent in this view of the west façade overlooking one of Olmsted's watercourses. A rugged retaining wall over seventeen feet thick at the base was required to support the massive house above. (Biltmore Collection)

one the private railway cars of the Vanderbilts arrived in Asheville: Mrs. William Henry Vanderbilt (George Vanderbilt's mother); brothers Cornelius Vanderbilt II, William K. Vanderbilt, and Frederick William Vanderbilt; and sister Eliza V. Webb, together with assorted husbands, wives, children, and necessary domestic servants—all to be transported by carriage up the private three-mile approach road that Olmsted designed to twist and turn through natural, wild forest. No hint of the house should intrude on this passage, according to Olmsted, "until the visitor pass[es] with an abrupt transition into the enclosure of the trim, level, open, airy, spacious, thoroughly artificial Court, and the Residence,

The grand staircase winds upward for four stories and is based on one in the Château de Blois, albeit spiraling in the opposite direction. Suspended in the middle is a massive wrought-iron chandelier with a tier of lights at the landing of each floor. (Biltmore Collection)

The Winter Garden is an area of sunken marble just off the main entrance, which is kept filled with flowers, palms, and ferns from Biltmore's gardens and greenhouses. The fountain is by the Viennese sculptor Karl Bitter (1867–1915). (Biltmore Collection)

Vanderbilt's scholarly interests are reflected in the library; its shelves contain over 20,000 volumes on forestry, gardening, architecture, and art, in addition to the predictable classics of a gentleman's library of the time. Easily the most magnificent room at Biltmore, the library measures seventy-three by thirty-four by thirty feet, the paneling is Circassian walnut, and the fireplace surround Italian marble. Karl Bitter carved the over-mantel figures of Demeter, goddess of the earth, and Hestia, goddess of the hearth. The cast andirons, also by Bitter, represent Vulcan and Venus. The ceiling painting is attributed to Giovanni Antonio Pellegrini (1675–1741); it was acquired by Vanderbilt in 1895. (Biltmore Collection)

The south bedroom, used by Mr. Vanderbilt, is paneled in walnut and hung with the prints he collected. The massive furniture is Spanish, Italian, and Portuguese in origin. The windows of this room look out to distant Mount Pisgah. (Biltmore Collection)

The breakfast or family dining room is one of the more intimate and appealing spaces in the house, with family portraits set against wall coverings of Spanish leather and Wedgwood "jasper" ware set into the fireplace surround. Although Biltmore was wired for electricity, a pair of silver kerosene banquet lamps illuminate the dining table. (Biltmore Collection)

On May 23, 1887, Vanderbilt purchased in Paris the sixteenth-century tapestries depicting the tale of Vulcan and Venus around which the baronial banquet hall was designed. Its arched ceiling rises seventy feet above the floor and the room itself measures seventy-two by forty-two feet. Like much of the furniture at Biltmore, the oak dining table and the canopied chair were designed for the house. Over the triple fireplace is Karl Bitter's bas-relief carving The Return from the Chase. The mounted trophy heads, animal-skin rugs, banners, and Gothic-style carving are all intended to lend a romantic air of medievalism to what is essentially a ceremonial space. (Biltmore Collection)

with its orderly dependencies, breaks suddenly and fully upon him." Today, as in the 1890s, this experience loses little of its impact in repetition; anticipation of entering the court from the forest grows with each turn of the road as it climbs to the site of the house.

With the house complete, George Vanderbilt married Edith Stuyvesant Dresser (directly descended from Peter Stuyvesant) in 1898. The Vanderbilts had one child, Cornelia, who married John Francis Amerherst Cecil; their son, William A. V. Cecil, is the present owner of Biltmore. George Washington Vanderbilt succumbed to a heart attack following surgery for appendicitis and died on March 6, 1914.

The year George Washington Vanderbilt occupied Biltmore, William Randolph Hearst moved from his native San Francisco to New York City, where he purchased a failing newspaper with part of a $7,500,000 gift from his mother. She had raised the funds by selling to the Rothschilds of London her interest in the Anaconda Copper Mining Company.

Like Vanderbilt, Hearst had been born to great wealth. His father, George Hearst, son of prosperous Missouri farmers, struck it rich in the Nevada silver fields. Shortly thereafter he married Phoebe Elizabeth Apperson and moved to San Francisco, where, on April 29, 1863, his son—William Randolph Hearst—was born. George Hearst promptly returned to the mining camps, and Phoebe Hearst spent most of her days indulging her only child. According to Hearst's biographer, "the child became the object of a flood of affection that engulfed him. He was mothered, loved, pampered, praised, protected, instructed, fussed over, waited on and worried about every moment of his infant existence." For

the rest of her life, Phoebe Hearst would be a strong influence on her son.

Eager to make her son a gentleman of culture, Phoebe Hearst took him on a grand tour of Europe when he was only ten, an eighteen-month journey through Ireland, Scotland, England, Germany, Switzerland, France, and Italy. This was no junket; tutors were engaged, Baedekers consulted, and according to his mother's diary, Willie commented that he would like to live in Windsor Castle and asked his mother to buy the Louvre for him. Anyone who has ever followed a ten-year-old around country houses and museums will not be impressed by this supposed precocity.

At prep school and Harvard, Hearst's academic career—according to one of his classmates—was one of "amiable indolence broken by spasms of energy." A period spent as the business manager of the Harvard *Lampoon*, however, whetted his interest in publishing, an interest cut short by poor grades and failure to attend classes. He consequently asked his father for control of the San Francisco *Examiner*, a lackluster newspaper the elder Hearst had acquired to advance his political ambitions. George Hearst reluctantly agreed. The year was 1887; the self-proclaimed journalist was not yet twenty-four.

No American newspaper publisher is better known or more controversial than William Randolph Hearst, whose journalistic career spanned more than half a century. Hearst was ruthless, cynical, and contemptuous of his readers. "The public is even more fond of entertainment than it is of information," he wrote in 1896. According to one of his more sympathetic biographers, he had "decided that the great majority of people, the masses, had no time or training for such a luxury as taste and could be reached and molded most effectively by the

Portrait in oils of Mrs. George W. Vanderbilt (née Edith Stuyvesant Dresser) by the ultra-fashionable, modern-day court painter Giovanni Boldini. (Biltmore Collection)

studios, radio stations, paper mills, and thousands of acres of real estate.

The foundations for the Hearst family land holdings had been laid by the patriarch, George Hearst. In 1865 George had purchased 30,000 acres of the Rancho de la

noise, sensation and repetition which he liked himself." The megalomania that drove Hearst, coupled with virtually unlimited financial backing, carried tremendous potential for good or ill. His controversial stands on such burning issues as free silver and war with Spain aroused fierce partisanship among both his supporters and his critics.

Debatable as Hearst's methods were, they succeeded. By 1917 he owned papers in San Francisco, New York, Chicago, Los Angeles, Boston, Atlanta, and Washington. By 1937 the empire he had founded fifty years before consisted of twenty-five daily newspapers, seventeen Sunday papers, wire services, magazines, motion picture

Oil portrait of William Randolph Hearst (1863–1951) by his close friend Orrin Peck, 1894. The next year, with $7,500,000 of his mother's money, the San Francisco publisher would take on New York City. (Hearst Monument/Ken Raveill)

shore-whaling fleet and the schooner traffic on which local ranching and mining operations were dependent to reach otherwise inaccessible markets. Throughout the 1870s George Hearst expanded his holdings; he also modernized the wharf on San Simeon Bay and erected

William Randolph Hearst and his wife, Millicent Willson Hearst, dressed for a costume party. Hostile biographers would later find significance in Hearst's choice of Napoleonic garb. (Hearst Monument)

Phoebe Apperson Hearst (1842–1919), a dedicated philanthropist, worker on behalf of women, and mother of William Randolph Hearst. (Special collections, California Polytechnic State University, San Luis Obispo)

Piedra Blanca (Ranch of the White Rock), once part of the land attached to the Spanish mission San Antonio de Padua. This particular point on the central California coast south of Big Sur, where the Santa Lucia Range sweeps back from the Pacific Ocean to allow the formation of a narrow coastal plain, has San Simeon Bay as a chief attraction — providing a safe anchorage for the

a modest two-story frame ranch house in an eastern pattern-book Stick style.

During George Hearst's lifetime, the ranch at San Simeon was occasionally used for family visits, which included pack trips by horseback to a spot they called Camp Hill. Sixteen hundred feet above the sea, the site commanded breathtaking views over the ranch to the

Julia Morgan (1872–1957), designer of San Simeon, shown here in a rare photograph with William Randolph Hearst. The five-foot-tall architect affected tailored suits and French silk blouses. "Mr. Hearst and I are fellow architects," she is quoted as saying. "He supplies vision, critical judgment. I give technical knowledge and building experience. He loves architecturing." In 1927 Hearst closed a letter to her with the signature "William Viollet-le-Duc Hearst, architect." (Bison Archives)

Pacific Ocean five miles away. Government mapmakers would later name this ridge Lone Tree Hill, but William Randolph Hearst would christen it La Cuesta Encantada—the enchanted hill. This became his Xanadu; here, at untold cost, he eventually built one of the most famous houses in the world, commanding an estate of 270,000 acres (over 400 square miles).

Following George Hearst's death in 1891, Phoebe Apperson Hearst took up residence at Hacienda del Pozo de Verona near Pleasanton, California. A formidable person who devoted much of her energy and financial resources to various good works, especially those advancing what today would be called women's issues, she was a founder of the General Federation of Women's Clubs, the National Congress of Mothers—forerunner of the Parent-Teacher Association—and the Travelers' Aid Association. Concerned that the growing number of women attracted to cities by jobs should have appropriate housing, she supported the YWCA movement.

Mrs. Hearst's charitable activities required an appropriate establishment for housing and entertaining guests. To expand the Hacienda, Mrs. Hearst called upon Julia Morgan (1872–1957) as architect. A native of San Francisco who had been raised in Oakland, Morgan entered the University of California, Berkeley, at the age of eighteen as an engineering student, there being no formal program of architectural training in the West at that time. Having determined on a career in architecture, she worked briefly for the architect Bernard Maybeck, who encouraged her to try for the École des Beaux-Arts, Paris, which was about to begin accepting female students in painting and sculpture. However, as Morgan later recalled, the French government had not announced whether women would be admitted to the Department of Architecture, "it not entering their heads that there might be women applicants. There was no preparation for such a case and no word against it; so I was given the benefit of the doubt . . ." and allowed to take the entrance examinations. She gained admission on her third try in 1898 and by 1902 had returned to America — the first woman to receive a certificate in architecture from the École.

In a profession in which women remain a minority to this day, Julia Morgan's success in Paris and her architectural career, which included the construction of nearly seven hundred buildings, is all the more extraordinary. Morgan recognized that she was unique. While she encouraged women by hiring them to work in her office, Morgan would comment in 1931 that "the few professional women architects have contributed little or

Early design by Julia Morgan (c.1922) for Casa Grande, on which Hearst has written in pencil: "I think there should be ten feet more width between the towers for the central gabled building. I think this will help rather than hurt the front elevation and it will be much better inside for the big assembly room giving that 85 ft length, and clearing the tapestries from above the doors into the refectory." (Special Collections, California Polytechnic State University, San Luis Obispo)

nothing to the profession — no great artist, no revolutionary ideas, no outstanding design." Such contributions, she believed, would come only when the number of women entering the profession had dramatically increased. Morgan never married and throughout a long and active professional life put architecture first. Dorothy Wormser Coblentz, who worked for Morgan, later remarked that "the pressure was terrible. She didn't realize that people had private lives . . . time meant nothing to her. She went out of her way to hire women, but expected them to emulate her."

Mrs. Hearst probably met Morgan during the time Morgan was working in Bernard Maybeck's architec-

tural office, before she left for Paris. Maybeck was designing a castle for Mrs. Hearst at Wyntoon near Mount Shasta at that time. Mrs. Hearst must have liked the young architect, for she even offered to assist Morgan financially while she was studying in Paris.

After returning to California, Morgan found her first professional work in assisting architect John Galen Howard during the construction of the Hearst Mining Building (1901–1907), given by Mrs. Hearst to the University of California, Berkeley, as a memorial to her husband. By 1903 Julia Morgan was enlarging and remodeling the Hacienda del Pozo de Verona for Mrs. Hearst.

Just as the Vanderbilt family settled on Richard Mor-

Hearst would write to Morgan in 1919, "The main thing at the ranch is the view." (Hearst Monument/ John Blades)

ris Hunt, the Hearsts chose Julia Morgan as their favorite architect; she would design and build for them some thirty commissions spanning three generations — homes, swimming pools, newspaper buildings, and radio stations. In the years before World War I, William Randolph Hearst had Miss Morgan design a villa to be erected at Sausalito, California, a scheme that was later abandoned. She also refurbished the *Examiner* building in San Francisco and a few years later designed a Mission-style newspaper building for Hearst in Los Angeles.

Phoebe Apperson Hearst died of influenza in 1919. During her lifetime, she had donated $21 million to educational and philanthropic causes. The chief heir to her estate of $11 million, including the San Simeon property, was William Randolph Hearst. Now the resources to build on a sultanesque scale became his.

After a quarter century in New York City and with his presidential ambitions thwarted, Hearst's focus had returned to the West. He could run his empire just as well from California, given improvements in postwar communications; and he was now plunging into motion pictures, in part to advance the career of Marion Davies, whom Hearst had discovered in the chorus of Florenz Ziegfeld's *Follies*. Hearst installed Miss Davies as the chatelaine of San Simeon, in effect replacing Millicent Willson Hearst (1882–1974), whom he had married in 1903 and who had borne his five sons. Hearst never cared much for social conventions, and after his wife refused to grant him a divorce in favor of Miss Davies, he lived openly with the actress for the rest of his life.

During the years that Hearst had been preoccupied with establishing his newspaper empire in New York, the ranch at San Simeon was little visited by the family. But during World War I he began to bring his children there. On one such occasion he wrote his mother:

We are back in our regular camp at the top of the hill. . . . I love this ranch. It is wonderful. I love the sea, and I love the mountains and the hollows in the hills, and the shady places in the creeks, and the fine old oaks, and even the hot bushy hillsides — full of quail, and the canyons full of deer. It's a wonderful place. I would rather spend a month here than any place in the world.

Shortly before his mother's death, Hearst visited Morgan's office and commissioned her to design a "Jappo-Swisso bungalow" at the ranch because — at the age of fifty-six — he was "tired of camping out and wanted something more comfortable on the Hill" to replace the usual cluster of sleeping tents around a main dining tent that was set up whenever he and his guests went there. How the bungalow with oriental or alpine origins became a sprawling complex that resembles nothing so much as an impossibly prosperous Spanish hill town is not clear, but the fact that Hearst came into his inheritance a few weeks after his first discussion with Morgan may have had some influence. The plan of guest cottages clustered around a central structure could have been suggested by the tenting arrangements, while the Mediterranean flavor of the entire composition may have resulted from Hearst's desire to take with him the Veronese wellhead that had given his mother's house at Pleasanton its name.

Morgan could design equally well in the wood-and-shingle Arts and Crafts style or that wonderful hybrid called Spanish Colonial. The latter blends the simple arches, courtyards, and tile of California missions with the Islamic wrought-iron balconies, and the white-stuccoed, sculptured massing of vernacular architecture that is common to many cultures around the Mediterranean. The Spanish Colonial style was much in the air since the Panama-California Exposition in San Diego (1915–16) had created something of a craze for Spanish Colonial Revival architecture, and books by Austin Whittlesey, Arthur Byne, and Mildred Stapley provided ample inspiration from Spanish sources. Hearst wrote to Morgan, however, that he found "California architecture . . . too primitive, and in many examples I have seen in Mexico so elaborate as to be objectionable." He continued, "I am not very sure about my architecture. . . . but after all, would it not be better to do something a little different than other people are doing out in California as long as we do not do anything incongruous? I do not want you to do anything you do not like." They

rejected following the Exposition too closely and ultimately settled on Renaissance architecture of southern Spain as the precedent, the towers of the main building (Casa Grande) being based on the church Santa Maria la Mayor in Ronda, twenty miles north of the Costa del Sol, which Hearst had visited and admired.

The focal point of the San Simeon complex is the cathedral-like Casa Grande surrounded by three guest "cottages." ("We refer to them as little houses," Hearst wrote, "but they are not really little houses. They are only little as compared with the big central building.") The entire La Cuesta Encantada site is roughly oval in shape; the main structure in the middle faces west toward

The three guest "cottages" nestle below the cathedral-like mass of Casa Grande, linked by interconnecting terraces and courtyards, creating the illusion of a Spanish hill town. (Hearst Monument/John Blades)

Casa Grande has what Morgan called a "fine 'looming up' effect" that dominates the complex. Inspiration for the towers came from the Cathedral of Santa Maria la Mayor in Ronda, Spain. (Hearst Monument/John Blades)

the ocean, across a broad terrace around which are arranged in a semicircle the guest cottages, respectively named Casa del Mar, Casa del Monte, and Casa del Sol — houses of the sea, mountain, and sun. Below them is the Neptune Terrace overlooking the most famous feature of the site, the Neptune Pool.

Actual construction began in 1920, but the three cottages with guest accommodations for only twenty-five to thirty people were not completed until 1924. And when Casa Grande was unveiled on Christmas Eve of the following year, it was still several years from its present form. Ultimately there would be 127 rooms in Casa Grande and the three guest houses (eighteen sitting rooms, two libraries, fifty-eight bedrooms, and forty-nine bathrooms). San Simeon, like Biltmore, is in a fairly inaccessible location, and Morgan, like Hunt, faced formidable logistical problems regarding the housing and feeding of hundreds of workmen and the transportation of materials to the site. "The San Francisco men sent down," Morgan wrote to Hearst, ". . . have nearly all come back, one turned back at San Simeon, some got to the top of the hill and did not unpack, and some stayed

The view from the Neptune Terrace across the pool and toward the Santa Lucia mountains. (Author's photograph) ▶

Work began on Casa Grande in the spring of 1922. The structure is earthquake-proof reinforced concrete faced with stone. The influence of Spanish baroque architecture is strongest here; the stark plain front sets off the antique limestone figures and modern cast-stone ornamentation around the main entrance, above which a cast-stone balcony stretches across the front. The dark ornamental roof between the towers is carved teak. In the foreground is a stone sculpture representing Galatea, the sea nymph, borne on the back of a dolphin. (Author's photograph)

The Neptune Pool, with its embracing semicircular colonnades and classical temple façade, did not assume its present appearance until the mid-1930s. It contains 345,000 gallons of water that were kept heated in Hearst's day. The Neptune and Venus figures are by the French sculptor Charles Cassou. (Hearst Monument/Ellis-Sawyer)

a week or more. They all agreed that the living conditions, money and food were all right, but they 'didn't like feeling so far away from things.' "

While Morgan designed and supervised, Hearst col-lected for the new complex. Much has been made of Hearst as an indiscriminate collector, the ultimate grand acquisitor, the man who bought everything that crossed his path and then hoarded it in warehouses, never to be

seen again. But Hearst's nonstop collecting was another sign of his mother's influence. Hearst's mother had been an inveterate collector for forty years — her gatherings of European paintings, furniture, and oriental porcelains filled the Hacienda in Pleasanton — and she encouraged similar instincts in her son as a hallmark of culture, not an uncommon *nouveau-riche* belief. By the 1920s, however, William Hearst's passion for collecting became nearly obsessive. War-ravaged Europe needed to sell, and

The assembly room in Casa Grande, as its name implies, served as the place where Hearst's guests could gather from the cottages and the upper-floor suites to savor the single drink he permitted to be served before dinner. Flemish tapestries line the room, which measures eighty-four by thirty-two feet. Morgan fitted the Italian Renaissance ceiling (twenty-two feet above the floor) with clusters of electric lights. The round plaque is by the Danish sculptor Bertel Thorvaldsen (1768–1884). (Hearst Monument/John Blades)

From the assembly room, dinner guests passed into the refectory, which is dominated by a French Gothic fireplace and over-mantel, Flemish tapestry, and Spanish choir stalls. (Hearst Monument/Ken Raveill)

The second-floor library, with its Spanish-Moorish ceiling from Aragon—actually three ceilings combined to fit this ninety-foot-long room—also contains Hearst's collection of Greek vases. According to Hearst, this was a room of "superior warmth and comfort." (Hearst Monument/Ken Raveill)

Hearst, collecting now for San Simeon and enriched by his mother's estate and the growing prosperity of his newspaper empire, dispatched agents, badgered dealers, and haunted auction galleries in a never-ending quest for objects to be loaded into freight cars and dispatched to San Simeon.

With its painted ceiling and walls hung with blue silk, the sitting room of the Doge's Suite is a typical Hearst pastiche of antique fragments. Over the sixteenth-century Italian fireplace is a terra-cotta tondo, surrounded by a wreath by Giovanni della Robbia (c.1469–c.1529). (Hearst Monument/John Blades)

Writing to one of Hearst's agents in Spain, Julia Morgan remarked wistfully,

So far we have received from him, to incorporate in the new buildings, some twelve or thirteen carloads of antiques, brought from the ends of the earth and from prehistoric down to late Empire in period, the majority, however, being of Spanish origin.

They comprise vast quantities of tables, beds, armoires, secretaires, all kinds of cabinets, polychrome

Hearst's private suite of rooms occupy the third floor of Casa Grande. The most magnificent of these is the Gothic study, which contains not only his rare book collection but choice ornamental objects of silver, bronze, ivory, and brass that are displayed in niches below the bookcases. (Hearst Monument/John Blades)

After forty-five films, motion picture star Marion Davies (1897–1961) wrote of herself, "All my life I wanted to have talent. Finally I had to admit there was nothing there. I was no Sarah Bernhardt. I might have been a character, but any kind of character. I had none of my own." This photograph dates from 1917, about the time she met Hearst. (Free Library of Philadelphia, Theatre Collection)

church statuary, columns, door frames, carved doors in all stages of repair and disrepair, over-altars, reliquaries, lanterns, iron grille doors, window grilles, votive candlesticks, torcheres, all kinds of chairs in

Four duplex suites were created at the back of Casa Grande; each contained a sleeping loft, bathroom, and high-ceiling sitting area. (Hearst Monument/Ellis-Sawyer)

quantity, six or seven well heads. . . . I don't see myself where we are ever going to use half suitably, but I find that the idea is to try things out and if they are not satisfactory, discard them for the next thing that comes that promises better. There is interest and charm coming gradually into play. . . .

Still, this is not the hoarding instinct of an elderly recluse fearful of never having enough. With San Simeon being only one of several building projects Hearst had under way in the 1920s, it made sense to him — since cost was no object — to buy everything that might be useful for his projects, leaving it to Morgan to select what ultimately might be needed for the complex. And gradually the quality of Hearst's acquisitions improved. He wrote to Morgan, "I have decided to buy only the finest things for the ranch from now on, and we will probably weed out some of our less desirable articles."

By 1924 the three guest "cottages" were complete and Hearst, now separated from his wife, began to spend more time at San Simeon, where he lived in Casa del Mar until Casa Grande became habitable. Gradually his life began to revolve more around the motion picture industry, and San Simeon gained public notoriety for its parties attended by Mary Pickford, Douglas Fairbanks, Greta Garbo, and Charlie Chaplin, although Hearst and Miss Davies also entertained the likes of Winston Churchill, Calvin Coolidge, and New York Mayor Jimmy Walker. According to San Simeon legend, when the Calvin Coolidges called for breakfast in their room, they were informed that there was no room service at San Simeon, everyone was expected to "come down" for meals.

Both the partying and the construction of San Simeon went on through the 1920s and into the early 1930s. While Hearst and Morgan planned further extensions to

the complex on the enchanted hill, the world slipped ever deeper into depression. The Hearst empire, drained of cash by the unrestrained life-style of its leader, found itself, by 1937, in debt $126 million. To avoid bankruptcy, Hearst at seventy-four had to relinquish control to a "Conservation Committee." Construction at San Simeon ceased, the purchases were halted, and vast quantities of

Julia Morgan made a particular specialty of swimming pools, and the eighty-one-by-thirty-one-foot blue-and-gold Roman pool at San Simeon is surely her most famous indoor effort. Puzzling how the "virginal and ascetic" Morgan could create such spaces, her biographer argues, "grasping the inherent sensuality of the act of swimming, she momentarily cast off her inhibitions to create a series of exquisitely engineered stage sets for hedonism." (Hearst Monument)

The tower of Casa Grande. (Author's photograph)

art and objects acquired at inflated prices in the 1920s — including an entire Spanish monastery in 10,700 crates — had to be sold. At the same time the Ritz Tower, Hearst's New York residence, was abandoned to creditors — no purchaser having been found — and his castle in Wales, on which he had spent an estimated $1,250,000, was stripped of its treasures and placed on the market.

San Simeon itself was saved from foreclosure by its unsalability. In the late 1930s, no one wanted to assume the burdens of a "castle" worthy of Ludwig II of Bavaria. In the meantime, the Hearst Corporation entered into an agreement with Gimbel's department store to sell the thousands of objects Hearst had collected; the store devoted an entire floor to these objects for a year. Hearst and Miss Davies continued to live at San Simeon until the fear of Japanese attack caused the house to be closed during the war. Briefly, Hearst returned in 1944 and work resumed after the war, but Hearst's health forced him to move closer to medical attention in 1947. He died on August 14, 1951, at the age of eighty-eight.

In 1958 the Hearst Corporation donated La Cuesta Encantada to the California State Parks System, which now operates it as one of the most successful house museums in the United States.

A F T E R W O R D

The story of the American country house does not end with Biltmore or San Simeon, even though it is unlikely that anything to equal them will ever be built in America again. For Americans of more modest means or less flamboyant ambition, the country house entered a phase of democratization, becoming the country home, seeking its inspiration not in palaces but in the smaller vernacular farm houses of prosperous yeoman farmers of Normandy and the Cotswolds or our own colonial past. One architect wrote in the 1920s, "There is . . . no type of European architecture so adaptable to our uses in America, as the English or Norman Country house. . . . The style is informal, and hence appropriate to our modern way of living."

The movement of prosperous Americans from the cities to the suburbs, made possible in the nineteenth century by streetcars and then trains that rapidly carried the successful businessman or professional out beyond the sprawling cities of New York, Philadelphia, or Chicago, was accelerated in the early twentieth century by the advent of the automobile. What might have been called a villa in the late-eighteenth or early-nineteenth century became a country home, an escape from the frantic pace and ugliness of the city into a fantasy world of a modern Arcadia. In the hands of architects like Robert R. McGoodwin and the firm of Walter Mellor and Arthur I. Meigs, this blend of English, French, and, occasionally, a bit of American colonial tossed in for good measure provided houses that appealed to prosperous twentieth-century Americans.

It didn't take the publishing world long to spot a fertile trend; *Country Life in America* began to appear in 1901, and from 1910 until the Great Depression *The Architectural Record* issued an annual number devoted to

Country house architect Howard Van Doren Shaw, FAIA, erected a house for himself in the picturesque Chicago suburb of Lake Forest, Illinois, in 1896. Shaw (1869–1926) was highly regarded in the Midwest for his domestic architecture, and his biographer says, "he was happiest when he was working with clients who wanted an American adaptation of an English country house." This view of Ragdale—Shaw's house— illustrated an article entitled "Color in Country Houses" that appeared in The New Country House (October 1917). (The Athenaeum of Philadelphia)

the architecture of country houses. The Architectural Book Publishing Company's annual *American Country Homes of Today* compiled the most recent works by country house architects from around the country, some of whom were also issuing self-serving monographs such as Arthur I. Meigs's *An American Country House* (1925), which recorded his design for Mr. and Mrs. Arthur E. Newbold—complete with ducks, chickens, and sheep to heighten the illusion of living a country life.

Eventually the Newbold house itself succumbed to

suburban sprawl. Too expensive to staff and maintain, the house and its outbuildings were sold and demolished, the fields cleared and transformed into a suburban housing development to realize the ultimate American dream of the country house for every man.

The Arthur E. Newbold house, Lavrock, Pennsylvania, by Mellor and Meigs was one of the most complete essays in the Norman French country house revival of the 1920s, including sagging barns, duck ponds, and enclosed livestock. (The Athenaeum of Philadelphia)

BIBLIOGRAPHIC
NOTE

A book as complex as this one — spanning as it does three hundred years of American history — is obviously based on the work of many scholars. Throughout the text I have attempted to suggest the source for quotations without the distraction of footnotes. As a further assistance to the reader, I have divided the following discussion of sources by chapter.

For a basic bibliography on American architecture the reader might begin with Charles B. Wood's chapter in volume 1 of Bernard Karpel, ed., *Arts in America: A Bibliography* (Washington, D.C., 1979). This will lead you not only to the main historical works, but to recent studies organized by region, building type, and architect. The best single source for biographical information on major architects is Adolf K. Placzek, ed., *Macmillan Encyclopedia of Architects* (New York, 1982). More detailed information on British architects is contained in Howard Colvin, *A Biographical Dictionary of British Architects, 1600–1840* (New York, 1978), and for those individuals who worked at some point in Philadelphia, there is my own *Biographical Dictionary of Philadelphia Architects, 1700–1930* (Boston, 1985). For a listing of buildings that have been registered by the National Park Service,

see the *National Register of Historic Places, 1966–1988* (Washington, D.C., National Park Service, 1989).

INTRODUCTION AND CHAPTER 1

The literature of English country houses is extensive. I quote from Vita Sackville-West, *English Country Houses* (London, 1941), but the general reader should be familiar with Mark Girouard, *Life in the English Country House* (New Haven, 1978), and the multivolume series by several authors — Christopher Hussey, James Lees-Milne, Oliver Hill, and John Cornforth — entitled *English Country Houses*, published by *Country Life*. Most American architectural historians have divided their discussions along chronological or geographical lines, leaving the reader to sort out the subthemes; unfortunately, it is virtually impossible to do more than skim the surface with any book that proposes to cover the entire sweep of American architectural history. Several standard works — even some of great age — remain useful as overviews: Fiske Kimball, *Domestic Architecture of the American Colonies and of the Early Republic* (1922 and subsequent editions), Hugh Morrison, *Early American Architecture* (New York, 1952 and subsequent editions), James Marston Fitch's two-volume *American Building* (1947 and subsequent editions), and William H. Pierson, Jr., *American Buildings and Their Architects* (Garden City, N.Y., 1970) all might be read and enjoyed by a general reader. More idiosyncratic, but nonetheless interesting, are Alan Gowans, *Images of American Living* (Philadelphia, 1964), and Roger G. Kennedy, *Architecture, Men, Women and Money* (New York, 1985). American architecture is brilliantly placed in a world context by Henry-Russell Hitchcock, *Architecture: Nineteenth and Twentieth Centuries* (Baltimore, 1958 and subsequent editions).

The first illustrated book on American country houses is William Birch's *The Country Seats of the United States of North America* (Springland near Bristol, Penn., 1808). On Birch, see Martin P. Snyder, "William Birch: His Philadelphia Views," *Pennsylvania Magazine of History and Biography* 73 (July 1949), 271–315, and the same author's *City of Independence: Views of Philadelphia Before 1800* (New York, 1975). On Hampton, see Charles E. Peterson, *Notes on Hampton Mansion* (Washington, D.C., 1970), and Lynne Dakin Hastings, *A Guidebook to Hampton National Historic Site* (Towson, Md., 1986).

On Adena, the essential works are Mary Anne Brown, "Thomas Worthington's Adena: The Frontier Replication of a Virginia Gentry Establishment," unpublished M.A. thesis, Ohio University, 1981, and Alfred B. Sears, *Thomas Worthington: Father of Ohio Statehood* (Columbus, Ohio, 1958). Talbot Hamlin's *Benjamin Henry Latrobe* (New York, 1955) and *Greek Revival Architecture in America* (New York, 1954) are still useful, although *The Correspondence and Miscellaneous Papers of Benjamin Henry Latrobe* (New Haven, 1984) is reshaping our view of Latrobe and neoclassical architecture in America. On Kentucky, see Richard S. DeCamp and Patricia S. DeCamp, *The Bluegrass of Kentucky* (Lexington, 1985), and for Tennessee, see Thomas B. Brumbaugh et al., *Architecture of Middle Tennessee* (Nashville, 1974).

CHAPTER 2

The classic studies of Virginia architecture are Thomas T. Waterman's *Mansions of Virginia* (Chapel Hill, 1945) and *Domestic Colonial Architecture of Tidewater Virginia* (Chapel Hill, 1947). Whenever a researcher believes he's discovered something new, it turns out that Waterman has been there before. His bibliographies and notes cover the earlier works, and for useful bibliographies of more recent research, see Calder Loth, ed., *The Virginia Landmarks Register* (Charlottesville, Va., 1987), and Mills Lane, *Architecture of the Old South: Virginia* (Savannah, 1987). Also useful are Marcus Whiffen's two studies, *The Public Buildings of Williamsburg* (Williamsburg, 1958) and *The Eighteenth-Century Houses of Williamsburg* (Williamsburg, 1960).

Many of the most famous plantation houses have recently been reexamined by young scholars, for example Mark R. Wenger, "Westover: William Byrd's Mansion Reconsidered," unpublished M.A. thesis, University of Virginia, 1980. Wenger has continued his research with articles dealing with various parts of the Virginia house, such as "The Dining Room in Early Virginia," *Perspectives in Vernacular Architecture*, III (1989) and "The Central Passage in Virginia: Evolution of an Eighteenth-Century Living Space," *Perspectives in Vernacular Architecture*, II (1986). On Shirley, there is Catherine M. Lynn, "Shirley Plantation: A History," unpublished M.A. thesis, University of Delaware, 1967, and Theodore R. Reinhart, ed., *The Archaeology of Shirley Plantation* (Charlottesville, Va., 1984).

Adding to our knowledge of William Buckland, there is Elizabeth Brand Monroe, "William Buckland in the Northern Neck," unpublished M.A. thesis, University of Virginia, 1975, which should be read together with Rosamond Randall Beirne and John H. Scarff, *William Buckland, 1734–1774* (Annapolis, 1958), and Robert C. Smith et al., *Buckland: Master Builder of the 18th Century* (Regents of Gunston Hall, 1977). On Rosewell, there are several modern studies: Bennie Brown, Jr., "Rosewell: An Architectural Study of an Eighteenth Century Virginia Plantation," unpublished M.A. thesis, University of Georgia, 1973; Claude O. Lanciano, Jr., *Rosewell, Garland of Virginia* (Gloucester County, Va., 1978); Ivor Noël Hume, *Excavations at Rosewell* (Washington, D.C., 1962), and Betty Crowe Leviner, "The Page Family of Rosewell and Mannsfield: A Study in Economic Decline," unpublished M.A. thesis, College of William and Mary, 1987. On Carter's Grove, see Mary A. Stephenson, *Carter's Grove Plantation: A History* (Williamsburg, Va., 1964), and Ivor Noël Hume, *Digging for Carter's Grove* (Williamsburg, Va., 1974). On several occasions I have quoted from Hunter Dickinson Farish, ed., *Journal & Letters of Philip Vickers Fithian, 1773–1774* (Williamsburg, Va., 1965), and Edward C. Carter II, ed., *The Virginia Journals of Benjamin Henry Latrobe* (New Haven, 1977).

Throughout this book I have linked economics to architecture. Economic causation for the American Revolution and the rise of Southern nationalism in the mid-nineteenth century is at best controversial, and I rejected it in my own doctoral research several decades ago, a position I've had no reason to reverse. Nonetheless, country houses are inescapably linked to the rise and fall of agrarian economies. For more such material, see John J. McCusker and Russell R. Menard, *The Economy of British America, 1607–1789* (Chapel Hill, 1985); Rhys Isaac, *Transformation of Virginia, 1740–1790* (Chapel Hill, 1982); and Eugene Genovese, "Slave Economies in Political Perspective," *Journal of American History* (June 1979).

CHAPTER 3

On villas, see David Bigelman, *La Laurentine et l'invention de la villa romaine* (Paris, 1982); and Clara Bargellini and Pierre de la Ruffinière du Prey, "Sources for a Reconstruction of the Villa Medici, Fiesole," *Burlington Magazine* (1969), and *Ancient Roman Villa Gardens* (Washington, D.C., 1987). On William Hamilton's Woodlands, see Richard J. Betts, "The Woodlands," *Winterthur Portfolio* 14 (1979), and Patricia Heintzelman, "Elysium on the Schuylkill: William Hamilton and the Woodlands," unpublished M.A. thesis, University of Delaware, 1972. Andalusia and Nicholas Biddle are discussed in Nicholas B. Wainwright, *Andalusia* (Philadelphia, 1976), and Thomas P. Govan, *Nicholas Biddle, Nationalist and Public Banker, 1786–1844* (Chicago, 1959). On The Solitude and Lansdowne, there are two particularly useful articles by Marie G. Kimball, "The Furnishings of Solitude, the Country Estate of John Penn," *Antiques* (July 1931), and "The Furnishings of Lansdowne, Governor Penn's Country Estate," *Antiques* (June 1931). Concerning the Binghams and their relationship to Lansdowne, see Margaret L. Brown, "Mr. and Mrs. William Bingham of Philadelphia," *Pennsylvania Magazine of History and Biography* 61 (July 1937), 286–324, and Robert C. Alberts, *The Golden Voyage: The Life and Times of William Bingham, 1752–1804* (Boston, 1969). Also useful is Beatrice Garvan, *Federal Philadelphia, 1785–1825* (Philadelphia, 1987).

There has yet to be a detailed history of Philadelphia architecture. Regardless of their age, Thompson Westcott, *The Historic Mansions and Buildings of Philadelphia* (Philadelphia, 1877), and Harold D. Eberlein and Horace M. Lippincott, *The Colonial Homes of Philadelphia and Its Neighborhood* (Philadelphia, 1912), still have useful material, although they have been largely supplanted by Luther P. Eisenhart, ed., *Historic Philadelphia* (Philadelphia, 1953), and George B. Tatum, *Penn's Great Town* (Philadelphia, 1961).

CHAPTER 4

For an overview of the Hudson River in art, there are several popular works, such as John K. Howat, *The Hudson River and Its Painters* (New York, 1972), and Raymond J. O'Brien, *American Sublime* (New York, 1981), but you might want to read some of the classic studies of American art, such as Edgar P. Richardson, *Painting in America* (New York, 1956), Jules D. Prown, *American Painting from Its Beginning to the Armory Show* (Geneva, 1969), or Barbara Novak, *American Painting of the Nineteenth Century* (New York, 1969). On the region's architecture, there are useful early works — Benson J. Lossing, *The Hudson from the Wilderness to the Sea* (Troy, 1866), Harold D. Eberlein and Cortland Van Dyke Hubbard, *Historic Houses of the Hudson River Valley* (New York, 1942) — and the more recent survey by John Zukowsky and Robbe Pierce Stimson, *Hudson River Villas* (New York, 1985). But as with the Philadelphia villas, there is yet to be a detailed study; most of the recent discoveries are to be found in individual house studies.

On the Livingstons, see Clare Brandt, *An American Aristocracy* (Garden City, N.Y., 1986), and George Dangerfield, *Chancellor Robert R. Livingston of New York, 1746–1813* (New York, 1960). On Montgomery Place in particular, see Jacquetta M. Haley, *Pleasure Grounds: Andrew Jackson Downing and Montgomery Place* (Tarrytown, N.Y., 1988). Anita Delafield, "Montgomery Place, the Home of Major and Mrs. John White Delafield," *Antiques* (1967) is charming, if not particularly informative. Joseph T. Butler, *Washington Irving's Sunnyside* (Tarrytown, N.Y., 1974), is still the best publication on that house, and on Otsego Hall see Harold H. Hollis, *History of Cooperstown* (Cooperstown, N.Y., 1976), and Louis C. Jones, *Cooperstown* (Cooperstown, N.Y., 1982).

On the careers of Andrew Jackson Downing and Alexander Jackson Davis, there is a new book jointly published by Dumbarton Oaks and The Athenaeum of Philadelphia: George B. Tatum, ed., *Prophet with Honor: The Career of Andrew Jackson Downing, 1815–1852* (Washington, D.C., 1989). Particularly useful are the introductory essays by George B. Tatum and Jane B. Davies's "Davis and Downing: Collaborators in the Picturesque." Fortunately, Alexander Jackson Davis's *Rural Residences* of 1837 has been reprinted (New York, 1980). Also important from the architectural historian's point of view is the chapter on Lyndhurst in William H. Pierson, Jr., *American Buildings and Their Architects: Technology and the Picturesque* (Garden City, N.Y., 1978), and for a curatorial point of view, John N. Pearce, "A. J. Davis' Greatest Gothic." *Antiques* (June 1965).

There is a considerable body of literature on Olana and Frederic Edwin Church. In particular, see David C. Huntington, "Olana — 'the Center of the World,'" *Antiques* (November 1965); Clive Aslet, "Olana, New York State," *Country Life* (September 1983); and Franklin Kelly et al., *Frederic Edwin Church* (Washington, D.C., 1989) which appeared after this book was completed. The latter — an exhibition catalogue published by the National Gallery of Art — has an especially good essay by James A. Ryan on the house and its meaning to Church.

CHAPTER 5

On the American expression of identity at the turn of the century, see Richard Guy Wilson et al., *The American Renaissance* (New York, 1979), the notes of which will lead the reader to the wealth of literature on the art, architecture, and worldview of Americans building palaces between 1876 and 1917. The most popular study of Whitemarsh Hall, Ca'd'Zan, Vizcaya, and several other houses of the period is James T. Maher, *The Twilight of Splendor* (Boston, 1975), which is also useful for its bibliography. The King Ranch is treated in two books, Frank Goodwyn, *Life on the King Ranch* (New York, 1951), and Tom Lea, *The King Ranch* (Boston, 1957). On the Newport houses, see Antoinette F. Downing and Vincent J. Scully, Jr., *The Architectural Heritage of Newport Rhode Island* (Cambridge, Mass., 1952, 1967), which is yet to be supplanted, although several authors have tried.

On Biltmore, see Wayne Andrews, *The Vanderbilt Legend* (New York, 1941), which is still fun to read. The best biography of the Vanderbilts' favorite architect is Paul R. Baker, *Richard Morris Hunt* (Cambridge, Mass., 1980), and on the landscape architect Frederick Law Olmsted, Laura Wood Roper, *FLO* (Baltimore, 1973), is excellent. Turning to Hearst and San Simeon, there is Sara Holmes Boutelle, *Julia Morgan Architect* (New York, 1988), the only full-length biography and the best single source on the Hearsts' favorite architect. On the house itself, I would suggest Taylor Coffman, *Hearst Castle* (Santa Barbara, Calif., 1985), an illustrated history that corrects several misconceptions about Hearst and San Simeon. Although originally published in 1961, W. A. Swanberg, *Citizen Hearst* (New York, 1986), remains the best balanced, full-length biography of Hearst, although Nancy E. Loe, *William Randolph Hearst* (Santa Barbara, Calif., 1988), provides an excellent and well-illustrated history of his life.

AFTERWORD

The best information on "country house for every man" in the early twentieth century comes from the periodicals of the time, particularly *American Architect*, *Architectural Review*, *Architectural Record*, *Country Life in America*, *House Beautiful*, and *Architectural Forum*; these contain such articles as architect Wilson Eyre's "My Ideal for the Country House: A House Expressing Domesticity," *Country Life in America* (May 1913). There is also a series of books, usually titled *American Country Houses of Today* published by the Architectural Book Publishing Company in New York City and written by such authors and editors as Frank Miles Day, Aymar Embury, Bernard Wills Close, Arthur C. Holden, Alfred Hopkins, Samuel Howe, and Alfred Busselle. On Howard Van Doren Shaw, see Leonard K. Eaton, *Two Chicago Architects and Their Clients: Frank Lloyd Wright and Howard Van Doren Shaw* (Cambridge, Mass., 1969). I've particularly focused on the work of Mellor and Meigs because they are so representative and their archives are at The Athenaeum of Philadelphia. The best overview of the firm is contained in Sandra L. Tatman, "A Study of the Work of Mellor, Meigs and Howe," unpublished M.A. thesis, University of Oregon, 1977. Arthur I. Meigs wrote an entire book about the Newbold House, entitled *An American Country House* (New York, 1925).

ACKNOWLEDGMENTS

Anyone who undertakes to write about American architecture needs to be familiar with two agencies of the federal government: the National Register of Historic Places and the Historic American Building Survey. The files of the National Register and the drawings and photographs of the Historic American Building Survey — the latter maintained by the Library of Congress — constitute the most complete and accurate body of information on American architecture. The staffs of both these agencies of the Department of the Interior were unfailingly helpful to me, and I particularly want to thank Robert J. Kapsch, Chief; John Burns, AIA, Principal Architect; and Jack Boucher, photographer — all in the HABS Washington, D.C., office.

For the researcher in seventeenth- and eighteenth-century American studies, particularly of the upper South, there are few libraries better equipped than those of the Colonial Williamsburg Foundation, nor could I imagine a more accommodating staff of professionals. I especially want to thank Pearce Grove, Director of Foundation Libraries; Mary Keeling, Architectural Librarian; James Garrett and Suzanne Brown, audiovisual librarians; and their helpful colleagues.

For guidance and hospitality, I must single out Nicholas A. Pappas, FAIA, Foundation Architect; and in the Architectural Research Department I am grateful to Mark R. Wenger and Willie Graham who generously shared their observations on the Virginia plantations.

The staffs and owners of every house mentioned in this book were unstintingly helpful. At Stratford Hall, I was fortunate to have the assistance of General John Wall, Executive Director, curators Elizabeth M. Laurent and Catharine J. Farley, and C. Vaughan Stanley, Librarian/Historian; at Gunston Hall, Donald R. Taylor, Director; at Drayton Hall, George M. Neil, Assistant Director; at the Charleston Museum, Mrs. Edward K. Webb, Coordinator of Historic Houses; at Middleton Place, Sarah Lytle, Director of Middleton Place Foundation; and at Biltmore House and Gardens, I want to thank William V. Cecil and his staff, particularly Susan Ward, Curator.

Moving inland, I am pleased to acknowledge Mary Anne Brown, Curator, Adena State Memorial of the Ohio Historical Society, Chillicothe, Ohio, for sharing her many years of research on that too-little-known house; Richard S. DeCamp, Director of the Office of

Historic Preservation for the Lexington Fayette Urban County Government, Lexington, Kentucky, and Patricia Storey DeCamp, artist and Kentuckian, who photographed Welcome Hall; Professor Daniel Fink, State University, Geneseo, New York, who took time from his own research into Genesee country architecture to photograph Hartford House and check information on the Wadsworth family. I appreciate the help of Milo V. Stewart, New York State Historical Association, Cooperstown, New York, for tracking down information and images of Otsego Hall and for mushing through the snow to rephotograph Hyde Hall. Thanks are also due to Bruce Cooper Gill, Curator, Harriton House, Bryn Mawr, Pennsylvania; John W. Kiser, IDEC, Associate Director, O'More College of Design, Franklin, Tennessee, for friendship and many favors large and small; H. Parrott Bacot, Director and Curator of the Anglo-American Art Museum, Baton Rouge, Louisiana, for sharing his expert knowledge of Mississippi River Valley plantations; and Janet S. Hasson, Curator, for help with Belle Meade Mansion.

For assistance with villas, I want to recognize David L. Reese, Curator, The Gracie Mansion Conservancy, New York City; Lynne D. Hastings, Curator, and Anna vonLunz, Assistant Curator, Hampton National Historic Site, Towson, Maryland; Susan Tripp, Director, University Collections and Curator of Homewood, Baltimore, Maryland. For help with Philadelphia villas, I owe a particular debt to James Biddle, master of Andalusia; Beatrice B. Garvan, formerly of the Philadelphia Museum of Art; Linda Stanley at the Historical Society of Pennsylvania and Kenneth Finkel at the Library Company of Philadelphia; and my former graduate student Mark Bower—now pursuing a successful career in historic preservation—who called to my attention William Morris's reference to a villa in 1795, which set an entire chapter in motion.

I depended on several people to lead me through the thicket of Hudson River villas, particularly the staff of Historic Hudson Valley, Tarrytown, New York: Joseph T. Butler, Curator, Jacquetta M. Haley, Director of Research—who generously shared her findings on Montgomery Place—and Laura Mogil, Public Affairs Coordinator, who found just the photographs I needed. Each of the houses I discuss in depth in the chapter has an overworked but dedicated professional staff that was always helpful: Cynthia Grant, who has the happy responsibility to be Site Manager at Montgomery Place; James A. Ryan, Director, Joel D. Sweimler, formerly curator, and Jane Churchill—all at Olana State Historic Site, who made several helpful suggestions to improve my discussion of that extraordinary house and its creator. Special thanks are due Susanne Pandich, Administrator of Lyndhurst—flagship property of the National Trust for Historic Preservation—and former curator of Biltmore, who provided substantial help with both those extraordinary properties; I also appreciate the assistance of Anne-Marie Demetz, Curator of Lyndhurst.

For securing photographs, I acknowledge the help of Angela Giral at Avery Library, Columbia University; at the Maryland Historical Society, Charles T. Lyle, Director; at The Preservation Society of Newport County, Mrs. Leonard J. Panaggio; at The Preservation Press, National Trust for Historic Preservation, Diane Maddex, former director, and Amanda B. West. In Florida, Charles B. Simmons and J. Kenneth Jones at Whitehall in Palm Beach and Patricia R. Buck at The John and Mable Ringling Museum of Art in Sarasota responded to my appeals. I also want to thank Roger L. Mayer for permission to reproduce a still from *Gone With the Wind*.

In the West, I'm pleased to thank James Steely, Deputy State Historic Preservation Officer, Texas State Historical Commission; Bruce S. Cheeseman, Corporate Archivist and Historian, the King Ranch; Catherine Rudolph, Director of Research, Santa Barbara Trust for Historic Preservation, and Michael Redmon, Librarian, Santa Barbara Historical Society, both for help with the de la Guerra house; Ellen Calomiris, Museum Administrator, Rancho Los Cerritos, Long Beach, California; and Larry Costa, Petaluma Adobe State Historic Park, who not only confirmed information but rephotographed his site at my request. At the Hearst San Simeon State Historic Monument, I am indebted to Sandra Barghini, Curator, who opened the gates, Robert Pavlik, Historian, who helped give dimensionality to William Randolph Hearst, and John Blades, photographer, who captured some of the magic of the last great American country house. For particular insight and assistance with the Julia Morgan papers, Nancy Coe, head of Special Collections at the Kennedy Library, San Luis Obispo, was quite helpful. And in finding just the right photograph of Marion Davies, Geraldine Duclow, head of the theater collection, Free Library of Philadelphia, could not have been more accommodating.

For over twenty years it has been my pleasure to be executive director of The Athenaeum of Philadelphia, a 175-year-old independent research library near Independence Hall that specializes in architecture and decorative arts. I am naturally prejudiced in favor of that venerable institution, but without the Athenaeum's collection and staff this book would not have been possible. In particular I want to thank Bruce Laverty, Gladys Brooks Curator of Architecture; Keith A. Kamm, Bibliographer; Ellen L. Batty, Circulation Librarian; and Eileen M. Magee, Program Coordinator, all of whom contributed to this project over several years. The book itself is a testimony to the designing skills of Joy Chu and Lucy Albanese. In the final analysis I probably would not have completed the book at all had it not been for the gentle—yet persistent—prodding of Channa Taub, Senior Editor, Henry Holt and Company, and the support of my colleague and wife, Gail Caskey Winkler, who had to bear the brunt of my frustration when more pressing matters took precedent over *The American Country House*.

INDEX